KOREAN BBQ

KOREAN
BBQ

MASTER YOUR GRILL IN SEVEN SAUCES

bill kim

with chandra ram

photographs by johnny autry

TEN SPEED PRESS
California | New York

Published in the United States by Ten Speed Press, an imprint of the
Crown Publishing Group, a division of Penguin Random House LLC, New York.
www.crownpublishing.com
www.tenspeed.com

Ten Speed Press and the Ten Speed Press colophon are registered trademarks
of Penguin Random House LLC.

Library of Congress Cataloging-in-Publication Data is on file with the publisher.

Hardcover ISBN: 978-0-399-58078-9
eBook ISBN: 978-0-399-58079-6

Printed in China

Design by Lizzie Allen
Food styling by Johnny Autry
Prop styling by Charlotte Autry

10 9 8 7 6 5 4 3 2

First Edition

To my parents, for taking a chance and risking everything to create a new life for us in America.

And to Yvonne—without you, I would never have had the courage to jump off this cliff.

Love, Billy

Introduction

I became a Korean American on a cold winter day in 1977, when my family landed in Chicago after emigrating from Seoul, South Korea. My parents decided to move us to America because they were worried for my brother and me. They wanted us to have more options and opportunities and thought America would provide them. But I didn't understand any of that when we arrived in Chicago. I was seven years old, I didn't speak the language, and I missed my friends in Seoul. In America, I was an alien: no one looked like me. I was miserable, and I just wanted to go back home.

I ditched my first day of school in Chicago. I grabbed my brother, who was six, and a book my Korean friends had filled with messages for me before we left, and we hid all day in the basement of the store where my family worked. Later, we found out the whole school had been looking for us, and I got into a lot of trouble. I had to apologize to the entire class and to the principal. After that, my parents took me to school every day for the rest of the year. They didn't trust me not to run away again.

I hated school that first year. I didn't understand what the teachers or other kids said to me, or what I was supposed to say to them. And then there was my name! My Korean name was Bum-Suk (and my brother's was Yu-Suk). Imagine going to elementary school and trying to fit in and make friends with names like that! All I wanted was a regular American name. That part of my childhood was hard, but I also cherish it in a strange way, because it's part of who I am today.

There were maybe only two other Asian kids in the whole school. I had to learn everything: currency, directions to the bathroom, even how to say hello. But slowly, it got better, and a year later, when more Korean immigrants came to our school, I was the one helping them get acclimated and guiding them through life in America. I didn't want them to go through the same trauma I had, and it made me happy to help others avoid it. When you are alone in a new country and then finally see someone who looks like you and understands where you come from, it's very comforting.

The experience was intense, but it showed me that if I could conquer a new school, a new language, and a new country, I could do anything. I got through it, and learned that the world isn't so bad, and that I could make it even better for others.

After living briefly with my aunt Janet, my parents rented a store and our family lived in the back, in one big room. We slept on mattresses on the floor and cooked on a hot plate; it wasn't too different from how we lived in Korea. We didn't feel bad for ourselves; it was just what we had, and we were perfectly fine with it. I earned extra money by picking up glass bottles to turn in for the nickel deposits.

I had some responsibilities as the oldest of five kids in the household (which included my three cousins), some of which were about food.

That's me—starting
out as a Korean baby,
but soon becoming
an all-American kid.

When we cooked and ate at home, our food was Korean with a lot of American touches. I had done a little bit of cooking before we left Seoul, including cooking my first cup of instant ramen over *seogtan* (burning coals) when I was just six. (Yes, my mom let me cook it without anybody helping me. Just remembering how dangerous that was makes me laugh. A little crazy, huh?)

My first kitchen duty in America was roasting sesame seeds and grinding them with a mortar and pestle for my mother's kimchi. Another of my jobs was carefully waving sheets of dried seaweed over an open gas flame to toast them for our snack. (Sometimes I'd put them in our toaster.) Also, every afternoon after school, I had to wash the rice, let it soak, and remember to press the button on the rice cooker so the rice would be ready when my parents got home.

But making our after-school snack was my real specialty. The fridge was loaded with honey ham, roast beef, bologna, and American cheese slices. Coming from Korea, where we didn't eat sandwiches aside from the rare luxury of a butter and sugar sandwich, having so many choices was heaven and meant that I could make sandwiches with all of the meats. I still make them today; at our restaurants we call it "phat style." I also had an infatuation with hot dogs: I ate them with rice, nori, buns, English muffins, anything, as long as there was tons of ketchup, and I still can't eat a hot dog without ketchup. (In Chicago, people go crazy if you eat hot dogs with ketchup, so I pretend the ketchup is for the fries but use it for the hot dogs. But keep that quiet!) I didn't know it then, but those early days of caring for my family with food was when I began the process of becoming a chef.

But my best food memories are from when we would get together with other Korean families to barbecue in the park. We were doing the most American thing, setting up grills, playing games, chasing one another, and cooking food, but our food was Korean. We were acclimating, but slowly.

As we settled into life in Chicago, we moved around the city a bit, each time learning about other cultures from our neighbors. We lived between an Indian neighborhood and a Jewish neighborhood, in an area where a lot of immigrants had landed. There were people there from all over the world, but we accepted one another. Then we moved to an Italian neighborhood. I remember the neighbors thought we were crazy when my mom strung fish on the clothesline attached to the pear tree in the front yard to dry them, right next to our clothes. To fertilize the garden, she buried fish heads in the soil—they had to be buried deeply to keep the flies away—and put crushed eggshells on top. Mom loved her garden; she grew sesame leaves (also known as perilla), Korean chilies, and little Kirby cucumbers to make kimchi.

I had a great time living in that house. My best friend, Tony Bruno, lived nearby, and we'd go to his house after school. Tony's family was as Italian as mine was Korean, but there were some similarities. Neither of our mothers spoke English, so we both understood what it was like to be the kid who had to translate conversations for his mom. Tony's family had a garden like ours, but they grew tomatoes. Instead of drying fish on a clothesline, they would dry, salt, and cure their tomatoes in wicker baskets under the sun. They even made their own wine (which, of course, Tony and I tried a few times). Looking back, I realize that Tony's life was like mine, just based in a different culture. It might have been fish drying out back at my house and tomatoes drying at his house, but we were both immigrant kids trying to figure out how to fit in and what it meant to be an American.

I got used to life in Chicago but I never really felt like I fully assimilated, especially at school, which wasn't for me; I was a very average student. In my junior year, school became a scary place for me, because that was when a lot of my friends picked the college they wanted to attend. Where was I going to get in? What would I major in? How was my family going to afford college? I had no idea. I went to the college night at the local junior college and saw the banners for all of the Ivy League schools—Harvard, Yale, Princeton, and Brown. I was about to walk out when I saw a giant white-and-blue wedding cake in the middle of the room, topped with a man in a blue tuxedo next to a bride. At first, I thought it was weird that someone was getting married at a college, but as I approached the cake, a representative from a culinary school asked me if I was interested in cooking. That was when I realized the cake was decorated to match the logo of the school.

A school for cooking? Was this for real? I had a million questions. What did I have to do to get in? What did my GPA need to be? How much did it cost? Even with all of these questions, I was relieved that I had found a path I wanted to walk. And I only found it after noticing that wedding cake. If I hadn't seen it, I don't know if I would be cooking today.

When I told my parents I wanted to attend culinary school, they were very supportive, but at the same time had no clue what that meant. I think they were just glad that I was going to get a degree in something. I decided to first enroll in the culinary training program at the local junior college, to save money and to stay close to home. No one I knew went to cooking school, so I was scared about wasting money, and this was an easy way to make sure a career in cooking was right for me. But once I started my classes, I knew I had found my calling. I went to

class and inhaled the smell of paprika, and of onions caramelizing in a pan. Those smells, the chaos of the day, tasting all of the food—it was a dream come true. Don't get me wrong; it was hard work. But I knew this was something I could make a career out of while following my passion for food.

I realized that I wanted to learn more and found Kendall College, a culinary school just outside of Chicago. This was my chance to finish my education without any limits; I even attended classes that I wasn't ready for, like taxidermy and advanced pastry. That was where I met my first mentor, Michel Tournier, this tiny Frenchman who moved around like a madman. He was very direct with everyone— there was absolutely no bullshit with him! I was scared of him, but I wanted to be in his class, so I snuck into his demos for the advanced pastry class on working with chocolate, pulling sugar, even cake decorating. They were at 4:30 in the morning, but his kitchen was alive. The smells of melting butter, caramelizing sugar, warm vanilla pastry cream, and croissants baking were everywhere, and it reverberated with the sound of eggs being cracked on a counter, oversized whisks hitting the sides of metal bowls, and a dough shaper shaking the floor as it rolled dozens of dough rounds at once. That scene was regularly punctuated by Michel screaming "You burnt the sugar, Sonny!" every time a student looked away from the sugar cooking on the stove and it went from caramel to black.

I loved that place. I didn't know many strong, direct people growing up, so when I found a teacher like Michel, I gravitated toward him, and we eventually became friends. When you don't have a lot of family in the country you move to, you adopt other people as your family. I soon started my internship at a French restaurant, Le Titi de Paris, but instead of going out with

At my graduation from Kendall College, with my mentor, Michel Tournier, and my mom.

the other cooks after working on Saturday night, I'd go home, get four or five hours of sleep, and then meet Michel for golf every Sunday morning. We'd play a round (a fast round—we weren't very good), then we'd go to breakfast and eat canned pâté with lentils and drink Merlot mixed with orange juice. I am not a big drinker, but I always looked forward to that drink. I could talk to Michel, ask him any questions about why he prepared something a certain way. We talked about the history of cooking, and he told me stories about his apprenticeships, like how there was no refrigeration back then, and every morning he would put all of the raw eggs in a big trough of water so any rotten ones would float to the top and could be discarded.

I enjoyed hearing those stories; they made me appreciate what I had. He had to leave his childhood home in Toulouse when he was fourteen to apprentice at a restaurant in Paris. He knew what it was like to move to a new environment when he was young, although I can't imagine what it would have been like to do that.

As I was finishing my apprenticeship and school, I read the book *Great Chefs of Chicago* and studied it like it was my homework. I wanted to work for one of the giants and set my sights on Jean Banchet. I left Chicago on graduation day for a job at Banchet's Ciboulette restaurant in Atlanta. Moving to a different part of the country and working for such a renowned chef was like another level of culinary school. It was great cooking at the restaurant, but I also fell in love with Atlanta and its food: Fat Matt's Rib Shack, Chick-fil-A, Krystal burgers, sweet

That's me, Charlie Trotter, and about $25,000 of truffles. Just another day at the restaurant!

tea, and pimento cheese. I'll never forget the sweet juiciness of my first Georgia peach, or my first American barbecue of rib tips in a vinegar sauce. I went from eating Korean food almost every day to eating American food, even if it was the line cook's classic quick meals of burgers, pizza, and frozen fish sticks.

I returned to Chicago a few years later and got a job cooking at Charlie Trotter's, one of the world's most exciting high-end restaurants at the time. Everyone was watching to see what Charlie did next; he set the trends for American fine dining.

Trotter's was a game-changer for me; the kitchen was like no other. We did daily tasting menus, sometimes changing the dishes daily. Hardly anyone else in the world was cooking like that. I was there when things were exploding for Charlie; he was opening a restaurant in Las Vegas and writing his first cookbook. During that time, I got to try the now-famous prosciutto made by La Quercia while its owners, Herb and Kathy Eckhouse, were still testing what they had learned in Italy on their pigs in Iowa. When Ohio farmer Lee Jones of Chef's Garden wanted to try growing specialty produce for chefs, I got to sample it before anyone else in the country. I'd call the venison supplier and request that the deer be fed figs so that four months later, the venison we served would have the faint, sweet undertones of the fruit. I couldn't have dreamed up a job like this one. I never knew what to expect on any given day, or what out-of-this-world idea Charlie would come up with and have us tackle. With Charlie, you had to be prepared for anything.

I planned to work there for a year and then go to South Korea and learn Asian cooking, but when my year was up, I decided to stay on. After a while, however, I was ready for something new. Although I had learned a lot from Charlie, the restaurant felt like a bubble. I never got to meet the customers and missed the feeling of taking care of people by feeding them. Also, I still wanted to find an Asian chef to work for. Back during my apprenticeship, I remembered the sous chef had come to me one day with a bunch of lemongrass and said, "Hey, how do I use this?" It boggled my mind that he assumed I would know how to use it. He didn't know I was Korean and not Vietnamese; to him, all Asians were the same.

I met chef Susanna Foo at a Masters of Food & Wine event because Charlie had asked me to help her prepare her food. But she didn't want anyone in the big kitchen to see how she worked, so we sat in her hotel room all afternoon filling dumpling skins and pinching them together, using the nightstand as our countertop. We were away from the kitchen and all of the famous chefs—and it was terrific. After that, she asked me to work with her at her restaurant, Susanna Foo Chinese Cuisine, and I realized that this was my opportunity to learn more about Asian ingredients from a great chef. I moved to Philadelphia to work in her kitchen, which was full of Chinese, Cambodians, and Mexicans; no one could communicate with one another, but it worked. And in her cooking, Susanna was putting cultures together in a way that felt entirely new. From her, I learned to season my food with soy sauce instead of salt, when to use coconut milk instead of relying on heavy cream, and how to use dashi to make sauces. It was yet another education for me. In French food, you reduce sauces to build flavor from the start, but in Asian food, you build flavors by adding something bright and fresh at the end of cooking. I was learning how to cook with lemongrass and other Asian ingredients that were both familiar and new.

But then, Charlie offered me the once-in-a-lifetime opportunity to return to Charlie Trotter's to be his chef de cuisine, so I went back to Chicago in February 2004. One day the follwoing year, I met a woman named Yvonne Cadiz. She had been the first female captain at the legendary Daniel restaurant in New York City, and she was spending a day working at Charlie Trotter's to see if it was a good fit for her. I introduced myself, then she looked at me for a long moment and asked, "What are you doing working here?"

That moment changed my life. Yvonne knew the instant she met me that there was something more for me to do. We went to a Cubs game on our first date and got married a year later, but that question she asked when we first met stuck with me. What was I doing working at a restaurant that served French-inspired American cuisine only to the people who could afford the most expensive meals? I spent half of my time with two phones glued to my ears, balancing one on each shoulder as I called to find out what our East Coast produce vendor was sending us before ordering the rest of what we needed from the West Coast. I felt like a stockbroker, not a cook creating the aromas and flavors I had fallen for when I learned to caramelize onions in culinary school. I wasn't creating food to make people happy like when I was a kid making English muffin pizzas to feed my cousins after school. It was a wake-up call for me when I realized that my family never came in to eat. It wasn't the kind of food or restaurant that they felt comfortable with.

When I was a young cook, I wanted to cook French food, and so pursued jobs with French chefs. I didn't think Korean food was as worthy as French food. But I eventually realized that my food was just as important as French cuisine. I didn't want to run away from being Korean, but I knew I wouldn't feel at home in Seoul anymore, either. I'm not just Korean, or just American. I just wanted to be myself, and cook my food.

I realized no one else was cooking the food I loved, so I had to do it. Korean food has redefined itself many times since I moved to America. Think about how many people believe it's about street food tacos! What a lot of people think of as "authentic Korean food" has changed, just as my cooking has evolved, as my life has taken different directions. What I do—adding the flavors of Puerto Rican *lechon* (roasted pork) or Vietnamese herbs or Indian tandoori—is authentic to who I am as a cook and as a human being. I want to harness the traditions of my childhood and take them to the next level. For immigrants like me, the food we grew up with is a legacy passed down from our parents—a legacy not only of the country they came from, but also of the act of sheer daring it took for them to move to a new country.

I wanted to cook food that reflected my heritage of Korea and Chicago, of kimchi and hot dogs. I wanted to share my experience of being from Korea, growing up in Chicago, falling in love with sandwiches, making connections with my Italian neighbors through food, navigating my way through culinary school and the French restaurant world, and marrying a Puerto Rican woman who introduced me to her culture and her table. I am not a formal person, so why couldn't my food be more like me? I wanted to continue working with farmers and sourcing the best ingredients while I re-created the flavors and fun of those family barbecues in the park. I'm a descendant of Korean culture, but it doesn't fully define me. People meet the food before they meet the person, so do there really have to be borders on our cuisine?

After answering those questions, a lot of debate, and a ton of work later, Yvonne and I opened our first restaurant, Urbanbelly, in August 2008.

We served noodles, dumplings, and Korean rice dishes. The food was as carefully prepared and the ingredients as rigorously sourced as at any fine-dining place, but it was a casual counter-service spot next to a Laundromat in a strip mall. The staff was just me, Yvonne, and my brother; we didn't have to impress anyone else. We opened on a Tuesday, thinking we could handle everything ourselves with just a couple of cooks and a dishwasher, but after a day of trying to feed the line of people snaking out the door, we had to hire four more people to keep the kitchen going. It made me so happy. The food and restaurant that were in my heart had come to life, and it was what other people— Koreans, Americans, whatever—wanted to eat, too. A couple of years later, we opened Belly Shack, our love story told through a hybrid of Korean, American, and Puerto Rican food, and then bellyQ, a modern Korean grilling restaurant.

Sometimes, I still feel like that kid coming home from school and soaking the rice for dinner while lining up a row of sandwiches for my brother and cousins. But now, as my nephews, Alex, Drew, and Max, become more and more American, I want to teach them about our family's culture and food in a way that makes sense to them. We've created a new world for ourselves, where our customers have become friends, like family, and I'm cooking my own version of what it's like to be a Korean American.

How to Kung Fu Your BBQ

So what does kung fu mean when it comes to Korean barbecue? And why am I using a Chinese martial arts term in a book about Korean grilling? Look, I'm still a Korean American kid who loves Bruce Lee movies. The kung fu masters in those movies could always find a way out of the toughest situations, even while they worked with apprentices, teaching them how to succeed. So for me, Kung Fu grilling is about adapting to your environment wherever you are and about passing your knowledge on to more people. It's about taking the ingredients you have on hand, the equipment you have to work with, and the time you have available and making the absolute best out of them for everyone around you. If you can't find water chestnuts at the store, use jicama; if you don't have a basting brush, use a bundle of herbs to brush sauce on your food. Kung Fu is the perfection of your skills through hard work, creativity, and patience.

When I think about what Kung Fu means to me in the kitchen, I think about the people who have had an impact on my food career, who taught me their ways: the Hungarian chef and Czech pastry chef who ran that first culinary program and who encouraged me to keep studying, Michel Tournier and his crazy screaming, Jean Banchet, Susanna Foo, and, of course, Charlie Trotter.

Charlie loved underdogs, which is why I think he picked me to run his kitchen. I try to follow his example and hire underdogs to work with me. I want to help my cooks succeed because a lot of people have counted them out. My cooking isn't about being strict or traditional; I'd rather be open to the ingredients and influences around me.

Cooking Kung Fu style is about not taking yourself too seriously or turning cooking into something that isn't fun. You don't have to know how to cook traditional Korean food to cook from this book. I want you to enjoy yourself and learn the fundamentals behind how to Kung Fu your grill, and that means making it stress free. I'll teach you the basics, but it's more important to me that you understand how to take what I've explained and create your own sauces and dishes. And most important, that you have fun. We're barbecuing here, so let's hang out, have a good time with family and friends, and eat really delicious food. That's what life is about!

The Basics

You don't need a ton of fancy equipment to have a great barbecue. Here's a list of what I consider my essentials, but don't feel like you can't make the recipes in this book if you don't have everything on this list. I've also included guidelines for handling the food and doneness temperatures; instructions on heating the grill and choosing your cooking method; and tips on cleaning up.

The Grill

What? You don't have a wood-fired oven in your backyard? Neither do I! In South Korea, people cook barbecue on grates placed over steel drums filled with burning coals. That's not a suggestion for you, but just a reminder that you can create delicious barbecue without a fancy grill. The recipes in this book assume you are cooking on a basic charcoal or gas grill, but you can even do it over a hibachi on a small balcony. And if it's raining, cold, the grill won't light, or you just don't feel like going outside, you can light the broiler in your oven. It's not the same as grilling, but it's what I do when it's chilly in Chicago and I want to make some Korean barbecue at home. Just be sure to preheat the broiler like you would a grill so that it's hot when you put the food under it, and to watch the food. Some recipes will take a minute or two longer to cook because the broiler won't get as hot as a grill.

CHOOSING A GRILL

Do you want a gas, charcoal, or wood grill? It depends on the amount of space you have, your budget, and how much work you are willing to do. Charcoal and wood impart unequaled smoky flavor, but when you want to make a quick dinner on a Tuesday night after work, you can't beat the convenience of a natural gas or propane grill. There are the specialty grills, too, like the kamado, a traditional thick-walled Japanese circular charcoal-fueled cooker, originally made of clay but now more commonly made of high-fire ceramic. Whatever type of grill you get, make sure you know how to use it and are comfortable with it. The best type of grill is the one you will use regularly.

Also, before you start grilling, always make sure you have more fuel—propane, charcoal, or wood—on hand than you think you will need. You'll be happy that you had that extra propane tank, bag of charcoal, or pile of wood when the grilling party goes a little longer than you planned. And if you use charcoal or wood, be sure to buy products that are not treated with chemicals. No one wants to eat a steak that smells and tastes like lighter fluid!

Tools

Always keep your tools in great shape. Store those that are grill-specific in your kitchen, not inside the grill or out in the sun and rain. Here is everything you'll need, along with a couple of good knives, a cutting board, wooden spoons, and assorted bowls and dishes.

FOOD PROCESSOR

You can do anything with a sharp knife, but a food processor will make mincing large amounts of ginger and garlic and mixing sauces go much more quickly. If you don't have one, consider buying an inexpensive mini food processor. It will cut down dramatically on your chopping time, and you can get a good one for about thirty-five dollars. It's not required, of course, but it will make cooking the recipes in this book even easier.

GRILL ACCESSORIES

You will need a handful of basic tools when you are working at the grill. You're going to be flipping and turning a lot of things, so make sure you have good tongs for turning meats and vegetables quickly and easily without losing them through the grate. I find the extra-long tongs with sharp, jagged-edged pincers that are often sold with grills hard to use, but if you're comfortable with them, you should use them. Just be sure to handle the food gently. I like long metal tongs with round, scalloped pincers. They act like extensions of my hands and allow me to handle hot food without crushing or tearing it. I never use tongs on really delicate foods like fish, however. That's when you need a spatula (or two) to lift it off the grill without breaking it. A sturdy spatula that allows you to flip everything from a shrimp to a steak without it bending is important, as is a meat fork that is long enough to reach over those dancing flames.

You'll need a couple of basting brushes for applying liquids to foods as they grill. I like to keep one brush for savory cooking and one for sweet. That way, I don't baste grilling peaches with the same brush I just used to brush fish with garlic butter. If you are nervous about getting burned while grilling, be sure

to have a long oven mitt and a thick towel on hand so you will feel comfortable and safe as you work. A thermometer is essential for checking the internal temperature of what you are cooking without having to hack at the chicken breast or burger to see if it's cooked; I like a digital thermometer because it quickly displays the temperature. Finally, you'll need a long-handled grill brush with metal bristles to scrub cooked-on bits of food from the grate from time to time.

GRILL PAN

A good grill pan is essential for grilling cut-up vegetables or other small items or for anything especially sticky or otherwise tough to maneuver on the grill grate. It will also make cooking entire meals on the grill possible. I like ceramic grill pans because they are lightweight and easy to clean, but you can use the same cast-iron grill pan you use on your stove top if you prefer. Just make sure anything you put on the grill is oven-safe. Let it get nice and hot before you add something to it, and make sure you don't crowd the food, or you won't get the nice char you want.

HEAVY-DUTY ALUMINUM FOIL

A few recipes in the book call for wrapping the meat in aluminum foil before it goes on the grill. This is mostly because the meat is coated with a sticky sauce that you don't want to get all over your grill, so make sure you buy heavy-duty foil and don't be afraid of using a couple of layers. Repeat after me: it is better to spend a minute wrapping things in an extra layer of foil than it is to take your grill apart and scrub sticky sauce off the grate or burners. Don't ask me how I learned this!

MANDOLINE

A mandoline is what we use in our restaurants to shave super-thin pieces of cabbage, carrot, cucumber, or just about any vegetable. If you have one, then you know how sharp the blade is. Never use a mandoline without the safety attachment—no one wants a salad with bits of your thumb in it! If you don't have a mandoline, an inexpensive Asian slicer works just as well, or you can even run a vegetable peeler down the length of vegetables such as carrots and cucumbers to create long, thin pieces.

Handle Your Food Properly

Here are a few things to keep in mind to make sure you are barbecuing safely. Take the food you will be cooking out of the refrigerator about 30 minutes before you want to put it on the grill. That way, it will lose some of the refrigerator chill and cook more evenly. But don't keep food at room temperature too long before grilling it, especially meats, poultry, and seafood. No one wants to be sick all night because he or she ate chicken that sat out in the sun for hours before or after it was cooked.

Be careful not to overload the grill with food. You should be able to see the fire and the grate when you are cooking. If you can't, you have put on more food that the grill can handle. Also, don't swab the food with too much oil. It will cause flare-ups and you'll have a cloud of smoke and a burned dinner before you know it. A light brushing is all you need.

Raw or undercooked meat can make you sick, so it is crucial to check temperatures when grilling (see "Doneness Temperatures for Foods," at right). Also, never put raw meat on top of a cooked item on the grill; the juice will drip down onto it, and raw chicken juice dripping on a burger can contaminate it with disease-carrying pathogens (and is no one's idea of a good meal).

After grilling, let meat rest on a cutting board or serving platter for 5 to 10 minutes so the juices will redistribute. If you cut into it too soon, the juices will run out, along with much of the flavor.

Learn the Temperatures

Two sets of temperatures are important, one for the various foods you will be grilling and one for the grill itself.

DONENESS TEMPERATURES FOR FOODS

You can try to get away with not using a thermometer, but you might burn a steak or two or serve an undercooked piece of chicken, which is why I highly recommend you have a thermometer (see Tools).

It is especially important to check the temperature when grilling chicken or pork, so you don't serve raw or undercooked meat (see "Handle Your Food Properly," at left). Here are the minimum recommended internal cooking temperatures for chicken, pork, and beef burgers and pieces:

Beef or pork burgers: 160°F
Chicken or turkey burgers: 170°F
Chicken or turkey pieces: 165°F

BEEF AND LAMB
Rare: 125°F
Medium-rare: 130°F
Medium: 135°F
Medium-well: 145°F
Well done: 155°F

PORK
Medium-rare: 145°F
Medium: 150°F
Medium-well: 155°F
Well done: 160°F

GRILL TEMPERATURES

Each recipe includes the temperature to which you need to heat the grill before you put the food on it. The best way to know if the temperature has been reached is to use the thermometer in the lid of the unit or hang an oven thermometer at the back corner of the grate, so it's not directly in the flames. If you don't have a thermometer, you can use this hand test to approximate the temperature: hold your hand, palm down, about 3 inches above the grill grate and time how long you can keep it there before it gets too hot and you have to pull it away.

High heat (500°F to 650°F):
2 seconds

Medium-high heat (400°F to 450°F):
3 to 4 seconds

Medium heat (350°F to 375°F):
3 to 5 or 6 seconds

Medium-low heat (300°F to 325°F):
7 to 8 seconds

Choose Your Cooking Method

Do you want to use direct heat or indirect heat? The answer depends on what you are cooking. Direct heat is quick cooking directly over the coals or flames, while indirect heat is slower and away from the heat source.

DIRECT HEAT

Direct heat typically results in grill marks and amazing charred flavors. It's like searing something over a stove-top burner set on high. If using a charcoal grill, you'll need to arrange the hot coals in an even layer; if using a gas or propane grill, you'll turn on all of the burners. With either type of grill, I like to close the lid while cooking; it keeps the grill from losing its heat, and helps cook everything evenly by containing the heat. I make an exception when I'm cooking something very thin or something fatty that might flare up while cooking.

FOODS TO GRILL OVER DIRECT HEAT

Meats and poultry that are less than 1½ inches thick, like skirt steak and chicken cutlets

Vegetables (unless they are very small or thinly sliced)

Small shellfish, like scallops or shrimp

Fish fillets or small whole fish

Tofu

INDIRECT HEAT

When using indirect heat, you usually start and/or finish the cooking over the hottest part of the grill to develop a nice sear and grill marks, but the rest of the time the food cooks away from direct heat with the grill lid closed. It's like cooking in an oven that isn't heated to the highest temperature but can still cook your food—basically like roasting or baking. On a gas or propane grill, that means turning off a burner or two; on a charcoal grill that means piling the charcoal on one side of the grill.

FOODS TO GRILL OVER INDIRECT HEAT

Whole vegetables like corn on the cob or heads of broccoli or cauliflower

Large shellfish like hard-shell crabs or lobster

Thick steaks, chops, or other cuts more than 1½ inches thick

Large bone-in meat cuts like shoulders or whole loins

Bone-in chicken thighs or breasts

Whole chicken, duck, or other poultry

Most fruit (the sugar content causes them to caramelize and burn easily)

Any foods treated with a marinade or basting sauce that contains a lot of sugar

Any foods wrapped in aluminum foil, including whole fish, vegetables, and meats

Keep Your Grill Clean

Before putting any food on your grill, get the grate super-hot—with hot coals if you're using a charcoal grill or with all the burners on if using a gas grill—to burn off grease remaining on the grates. Scrub the grates with your grill brush to remove any bits of food and grease. If you have a gas grill, you can do this after you have finished grilling, so it is ready to go the next time you want to grill. This helps maintain your grill, but it's not the same as cleaning it. If you use your grill regularly, you should deep clean it every other month. Remove the grate and the drip pan (if your grill has one), soak them in soapy water, and then scrub them to remove all the excess grease. If you are using a charcoal grill, be sure to clean the ash grill tray so the excess ashes don't blow around. Keeping your grill clean will help prevent both flare-ups and your food from tasting like old grease. And whenever possible, keep your grill covered and protected from Mother Nature. Snow, rain, and wind can cause damage (I know this from experience, living in Chicago). You'll be able to enjoy your grill a lot longer if you take care of it.

Keep It Fun

Remember, grilling should be fun. Always. It's a rule. Keep a cold beverage in your hand and family and friends nearby. Standing at a grill laughing with friends is one of the best ways to cook. Don't let the food burn, but don't worry too much about the rules, either.

The Korean BBQ Pantry

You know what a lot of people find intimidating about Korean—or Asian—cooking? The basic ingredients. Some are spicy, some are pungent; they might look or sound or smell weird. But don't worry: you won't need to spend a lot of time or money hunting these down. I've cut the list to a handful of basics that will help you make dozens of dishes and have even included some non-Korean ingredients that will make the flavors in your food pop. I've also listed a few sauces and spice pastes you can buy. This might seem like cheating, but Asian chefs and home cooks almost never make those things themselves. They buy them so they don't have to sweat over their stove for hours, or even days. Most of these pantry items are available at regular grocery stores, but if you have trouble finding them, you can always order them online. I look for spices on Amazon; they seem to have everything.

The Traditional Korean BBQ Pantry

We'll start with the traditional ingredients used in Korean barbecue. Here are the ones I find essential in my cooking.

GOCHUJANG

This is a fermented Korean chili paste made from red chilies, starchy rice, fermented soybeans, and salt. It is brick red and thick like miso and is sold in a tub, not in a tube or jar. *Gochujang* tastes a little sweet and a little salty, with a hint of fermented flavor, and the combination means it packs a punch. A little goes a long way—trust me! You'll find a numbered heat scale on the back of some containers. Go for level 3, which is midlevel spicy, and you should be in good shape. I like to smear a dab of *gochujang* on a pork bun, sandwich, or taco, or add a spoonful to any stew or chili to boost the flavors.

KOREAN CHILI FLAKES, AKA GOCHUGARU

First things first: Korean chili flakes are not the same as the red pepper flakes you put on your pizza (though you could definitely put Korean chili flakes on pizza and it would be *delicious*). Korean chili flakes don't include seeds, so they don't pack the same heat intensity as red pepper flakes. That's not to say they taste sweet, but rather that they have the aromatics of chilies, an earthy flavor, and only gentle heat. I use coarsely ground Korean chili flakes in my cooking.

SOY SAUCE

Soy sauce is typically made from fermented soybeans, wheat, and brine, and for Asian cooks like me, it's our salt. There are many types of soy sauce, all with different levels of flavor intensity, sold in stores and online. Kikkoman brand or the standard soy sauce stocked in your supermarket will work for any recipe in this book.

My wife, Yvonne, is, like a lot of people, gluten intolerant. I want to make sure she can always eat what I'm cooking, so I use tamari, which is made with little or no wheat (check the label to make sure it is completely wheat free if you need that). It is actually the original Japanese soy sauce, as its recipe is closest to the soy sauce introduced by the Chinese to Japan. Although It is darker in color and richer in flavor than regular soy sauce, you can use them interchangeably in this book.

TOFU

Okay, bear with me, people! I know tofu has the reputation of having no flavor, but you will be seasoning it with spices and glazes and you won't believe how tasty it is. Tofu is a high-protein vegetarian product made from soy milk, and comes in two main types. Silken tofu is made by pouring the coagulated soy milk into molds, where it sets but is never pressed. It has a smooth, delicate, "silky" texture and comes in soft, firm, and extra-firm densities. Block tofu is made by simmering the coagulated soy milk until the curds and whey separate, then transferring it to molds and pressing it. It is sold in four main consistencies, depending on how much of the whey has been pressed out: soft tofu, which has a custard-like texture and is good for blending into sauces; medium tofu, which has a firmer texture and works for braised dishes but will fall apart if grilled or fried; and firm and extra-firm tofu, which are good to use when you want to stir-fry or grill. Always thoroughly drain tofu before using it. You can place it between a few paper towels and gently press it to release the excess water. To store leftover uncooked tofu, immerse it in fresh water in a covered container and refrigerate it, changing the water once a day. (It will keep for a few days.) You can also freeze leftover tofu, which is handy if you've bought a big block of it. Cut it into pieces before you freeze it so you

don't have to thaw out the whole block when you want to use it.

When I discovered tofu cream cheese, it proved a game-changer for me because I'm allergic to dairy products. I was skeptical at first, but after trying it in a few recipes, I'm now a very happy convert, because it means I can have creamy dips and sauces again. I use Tofutti brand in my cooking at home and at our restaurants.

TOGARASHI

This is the stuff! *Togarashi*, or *shichimi togarashi* as it's also known, is a peppery, complex Japanese blend of seven spices. The amount of each ingredient will vary depending on the brand you buy, but it always has ground dried chilies, dried orange peel, dried garlic, ground nori, sesame seeds, and hemp seeds. I use it to season grilled meats and vegetables, but you can use it on anything. Try sprinkling a little on popcorn or French fries for an extra pop of flavor. When you shop for it, make sure to ask for *shichimi togarashi*. Do not go home with *ichimi togarashi*, which are just chili flakes. Make sure you get the real thing.

The Not-So-Traditional Korean BBQ Pantry

After living in America and working in different cities as a cook, I discovered some other ingredients essential to my cooking that are just as important as the traditional Korean ones. Here are a few essential to my grilling.

CHILI POWDER

Chili powder is a ground blend of different chilies, plus spices like cumin, paprika, garlic, and oregano. You probably have a container or two of chili powder in your kitchen right now, but if it's old, it won't have much flavor. Take a big sniff, if you can't smell much of anything (and if it doesn't make you sneeze), it's time to toss it and get a fresh jar.

CURRY POWDER

People are often confused about curry. They don't know whether it's a stewed dish or a seasoning, whether it's spicy or mild, or even whether it's bright yellow, red, or another color. When I talk about curry, I am talking about curry powder, which in my kitchen is simply the name for an Indian blend of around twenty spices and seeds, most often including cardamom, chili, cinnamon, cloves, coriander, cumin, fennel seeds, fenugreek, mace, nutmeg, black pepper, poppy and sesame seeds, saffron, tamarind, and finally, turmeric, which gives the powder its golden color. I like to use a Madras curry powder, which is typical of southern India, because it has a little heat to it. Trong Food brand Madras curry powder is a good one.

FISH SAUCE

If there is anything as funky as the smell of fish sauce straight from the bottle . . . yeah, I don't want to know about it. Fish sauce is made from anchovies that are salted and left to ferment and age. If you take a whiff from the bottle, it's all old fish, but when you cook with it, you don't taste anything like that. Fish sauce just hangs out in the background, providing a huge umami flavor that basically turns up the volume on whatever you have just made. It's used throughout Southeast Asia as a flavoring or as the base for dipping sauces. I use more fish sauce than soy sauce, as it really intensifies the flavor of whatever I am making. Look for *nuoc mam* (the Vietnamese name) or *nam pla* (the Thai name) on the bottle label. I go through loads of Three Crabs brand fish sauce in my kitchen.

GREEK YOGURT

Yogurt is a tangy, rich way to thicken a sauce or marinade so it will cling to the food. I like

it as a marinade because the lactic acid in it gently tenderizes meats. I prefer full-fat Greek yogurt, which is thicker and has a tangier flavor than regular yogurt. If you can't find Greek yogurt, buy regular plain yogurt, line a colander or strainer with cheesecloth, a coffee filter, or even a thick paper towel, place the strainer over a bowl, scoop the yogurt into it, and leave the yogurt to drain in the refrigerator for 3 or 4 hours, until it thickens.

HOISIN SAUCE

In some ways, hoisin sauce resembles American barbecue sauce: it's a thick, dark, strong-flavored sauce that is perfect for basting meats on the grill. That comparison ends with their ingredients lists, however. Hoisin is made from soybeans, sesame seeds, chilies, garlic, sugar, vinegar, and various spices. Look for it in jars in Asian markets and most supermarkets.

KAFFIR LIME LEAVES

These leaves are like perfume to me. Their aroma is delicate and floral, yet they have an intense citrusy flavor. I like to use them whole to infuse flavor in soups and sauces. I crush them in my hand before adding them to the pot, as it helps release their essential oils, imparting even more flavor. What they will contribute to your cooking is worth the effort of seeking them out. Look for them fresh in Asian markets. If you discover a batch of good fresh ones, buy more than you need and stash some in your freezer for times when they are harder to find. Don't bother with the dried ones; they don't have much flavor.

LEMONGRASS

Prized in Southeast Asian (especially Thai and Vietnamese) cuisine for its subtle lemon aroma, lemongrass adds brightness, rather than a strong citrus flavor, to a dish. It can be found frozen, dried and powdered, or fresh and is used in beverages, soups, and curries.

To use fresh lemongrass, cut the dry, grassy few inches off the top, trim the root from the bottom, peel away and discard the tough outer layers from the bulb, and mince or slice as directed in individual recipes. You can also put a piece of the stalk in the pot to infuse flavor; just pull it out before you serve.

MIRIN
A Japanese rice wine similar to sake but with a lower alcohol content, mirin is a sweet cooking wine with just enough acid to balance the sweetness. I like it for its mellow flavor and use it in marinades, dipping sauces, and dressings.

SAMBAL OELEK
Made from chilies, salt, and vinegar, sambal oelek, a staple of the Indonesian kitchen, is a bright red chili sauce. It is loaded with seeds from the chilies used to make it, and it adds both heat and acid to recipes. I like it because it's a huge base of flavor for any dish and lets me cut down on the amount of salt I need to add. If you can't find sambal oelek but have access to Thai chilies, just puree them with a little vinegar and salt.

SESAME OIL
There are two basic types of sesame oil. One is light in color and flavor and has deliciously nutty nuances. It's excellent for everything from salad dressings to sautéing. The darker toasted sesame oil is made from roasted sesame seeds, which gives it a much stronger taste and fragrance. It's best used as a flavor accent rather than as a cooking oil, as some of its character is lost when it is heated. Because we go through a lot of sesame oil at our restaurants, we keep it in the pantry. But if you are not using it every day, keep your bottle in the refrigerator or in a cool, dark place so it doesn't turn rancid. It will thicken and become cloudy in the refrigerator, so be sure to pull it out and give it time to "melt" to room temperature before using it. It doesn't take long. I use Kadoya brand sesame oil in my kitchen.

SWEET CHILI SAUCE
Like the name says, sweet chili sauce is made from a blend of chilies and some type of sweetener, either fruit (plum) or a refined sugar. You can use it straight from the bottle as a dipping sauce for fried chicken or egg rolls. I use it as part of a marinade or basting sauce in grilling recipes when I want a sticky, sweet glaze; the sugars in the sauce caramelize nicely. I prefer the Mae Ploy brand.

YUZU
Grown mostly in Korea, Japan, and China, yuzu is a round, yellow, fragrant citrus fruit used in cooking. It is difficult to find fresh, but you can buy yuzu juice in most Asian markets or online. I use the zest from the peel and the juice in my cooking. Its flavor and aroma are floral and citrusy, like a cross between grapefruit and lemon or lime, though it's not as sharp or acidic. Although yuzu juice is less tart than lemon or lime juice, you can substitute either of them if you can't find yuzu juice. You might see *yuzu kosho* at the grocery store, which is a paste made from chilies fermented with salt and mixed with yuzu zest and juice.

As you can see, I don't have any problems incorporating new or nontraditional ingredients into my barbecue pantry, and neither should you. This is what I consider essential, but you should add your favorite ingredients to your own pantry. If you have a special love for a spice like cumin, or for the tang of Dijon mustard, keep some on hand and use it in your cooking.

Master Sauces and Seasonings

In French cooking, you have the mother sauces, like béchamel and hollandaise, which are the building blocks of classic French cuisine— the foundations for other sauces or dishes. Each mother sauce is the basis to make several more sauces; you just have to add an ingredient or two. Korean barbecue master sauces are nothing like French mother sauces in style or flavor, but they serve the same purpose: acting as a flavor foundation for the dish and a starting-off point to make more sauces, marinades, and dressings.

This chapter is where you'll learn my Korean barbecue master recipes: seven sauces and three spice mixes that form the flavor base for many of the recipes in this book. Chefs always make sure they have all of the little things prepared in advance, so when they are ready to cook,

everything comes together quickly and easily. These master sauces and spice mixtures are designed to be made in advance, to make your cooking easier and more relaxed and fun, which is what Korean barbecue should be. Each recipe offers a different flavor profile and can be used in different ways: as a marinade, salad dressing, dipping sauce, glaze, or spread. I also add different ingredients to the sauces to change the flavors and create new sauces. You'll see that I've listed the main flavors present in each master sauce recipe to give you an idea of the flavor profile of each sauce before you make it. You can also use this as a reference for when you want to use these sauces to create something new. How do you do that? By tasting everything, and thinking about how to combine the flavors in a way that tastes good to you. For example, pork has a bit of sweetness to it, so if you were creating a new pork dish you could think about if you want to accent the sweetness by pairing it with a sweet sauce like the Korean BBQ Sauce (page 34), or contrast the sweetness with a tangier sauce like the Nuoc Cham Sauce (page 42).

Each master recipe includes a list of all of the recipes in the book that call for it. That way, you can always plan a meal according to what sauce or spice mixture you have ready. But because these master recipes are so easy to prepare, I suggest you take an hour or two one afternoon to make all of them (this is when you'll be really happy you have a food processor), then stash them in your fridge or freezer. You can freeze small portions of them in ice cube trays or little containers so you're ready to fire up the grill on a weeknight, for an impromptu Sunday lunch, or whenever the mood hits.

Each master recipe is also color coded with its own unique color. Whenever a master recipe is used in another recipe in the book, it's

marked with that color along with a cross-reference for faster and easier identification. There is also a color-coded cheat sheet of all the master recipes inside the front and back covers of the book.

Having these master sauces and spice mixtures ready to go is how I create menus and cook in our restaurants. It helps them run smoothly and guarantees the food is consistently delicious, but it also allows me to train inexperienced cooks. I remember how Charlie Trotter liked to give underdogs a chance, and I try to do the same in our restaurants by hiring people who have been through a rough patch, who maybe have been in prison or unemployed for a long time. Some of them don't fit into society, in the same way I didn't fit into school when I was a kid. This is how I can give them the kind of opportunity that I got when my parents moved our family to America. These workers don't come to me as Korean barbecue masters, but with this system of master sauce recipes, they can quickly and easily learn how to cook Korean barbecue and develop the skills to become better cooks. And you can, too.

I also use these sauces and spices at home. I like to plan ahead because it's the only way I can be sure I have food at home to cook for dinner. (I know it sounds weird for a chef to say that, but chefs don't cook like chefs when we're at home. We're as desperate for an easy dinner as anyone else.) I sometimes buy extra meat and make more of the master sauces than I need that day. Then I portion out enough meat for one or two meals, add enough sauce to marinate it, put it in a plastic freezer bag, and freeze it. On the day I want to cook it, I just pull it out of the freezer in the morning and it's ready to hit the grill at dinnertime. Trust me, life is a lot spicier and fun when you have Korean barbecue waiting in your freezer.

What about salt?

These sauces have so much flavor (and salt from the soy sauce and fish sauce) that you'll find you don't need to use much—if any—extra salt on the meat, seafood, vegetables, or tofu you are cooking. I like to keep some good kosher salt on hand in case I need it after the food is cooked, but when using the master sauces and spice mixtures, you don't need to salt your food for the grill like you would if you were cooking a traditional steak or burger.

Korean BBQ Sauce

GINGER

NUTTY SESAME

SWEET

I learned the essence of American barbecue when I worked as a cook in Atlanta, and I still crave that sticky, smoky, tender meat. We capture those memories when we cook with this sauce at our restaurants. With sweetness coming from the brown sugar, kiwi, and pear, plus the sharpness from the onion, soy sauce, and garlic, this sauce has everything you need for barbecue with a Korean touch. I always give credit to my mom for this recipe because she showed me how to make it. Over the years, I've made some modifications to take it to the next level, but don't tell her! She believes that I am still using the same recipe she taught me all those years ago.

1 cup dark brown sugar, firmly packed
½ cup water
1 cup soy sauce
1 small white onion, coarsely chopped
1 Asian pear, peeled and coarsely chopped
1 kiwi, peeled and coarsely chopped
8 cloves garlic, peeled
1 (1-inch) piece fresh ginger, peeled and sliced
¼ cup toasted sesame oil

PREP TIME 20 minutes
MAKES 4 cups

Combine the brown sugar, water, and soy sauce in a bowl and whisk until the sugar dissolves. Transfer the mixture to a food processor, add the onion, pear, kiwi, garlic, and ginger, and process for about 2 minutes, until completely smooth. Add the sesame oil and blend until fully combined.

Transfer to an airtight container and refrigerate for up to 2 weeks or freeze for up to 2 months. Or freeze in standard ice cube trays, then transfer the cubes (they'll be about 2 tablespoons each) to plastic freezer bags and freeze for up to 2 months.

Korean BBQ Sauce

Lemongrass Chili Sauce

CITRUSY
SWEET
GENTLE HEAT

The inspiration for this recipe came from a trip to Thailand I took a few years ago. Those sweet, spicy, citrusy flavors come right back to me every time I make it. You can use this sauce for braising chicken or for making dipping sauces or glazes for fried appetizers, but I like it best for barbecue. It's thick enough to cling to the meat, adds a good char from all the sugars that caramelize on the grill, and delivers the spicy, fresh flavors of Thailand.

1 teaspoon minced garlic

1 teaspoon minced, peeled fresh ginger

¼ cup minced lemongrass

1 cup sweet chili sauce

¼ cup fish sauce

¼ cup sambal oelek

2 tablespoons toasted sesame oil

PREP TIME 10 minutes
MAKES 2¼ cups

——

Combine the garlic, ginger, lemongrass, chili sauce, fish sauce, sambal oelek, and oil in a bowl and whisk until blended. Transfer to an airtight container and refrigerate for up to 2 weeks or freeze for up to 2 months (see note).

NOTE This sauce won't fully harden when frozen, so you can spoon out as much as you need whenever you want to use it.

Lemongrass Chili Sauce

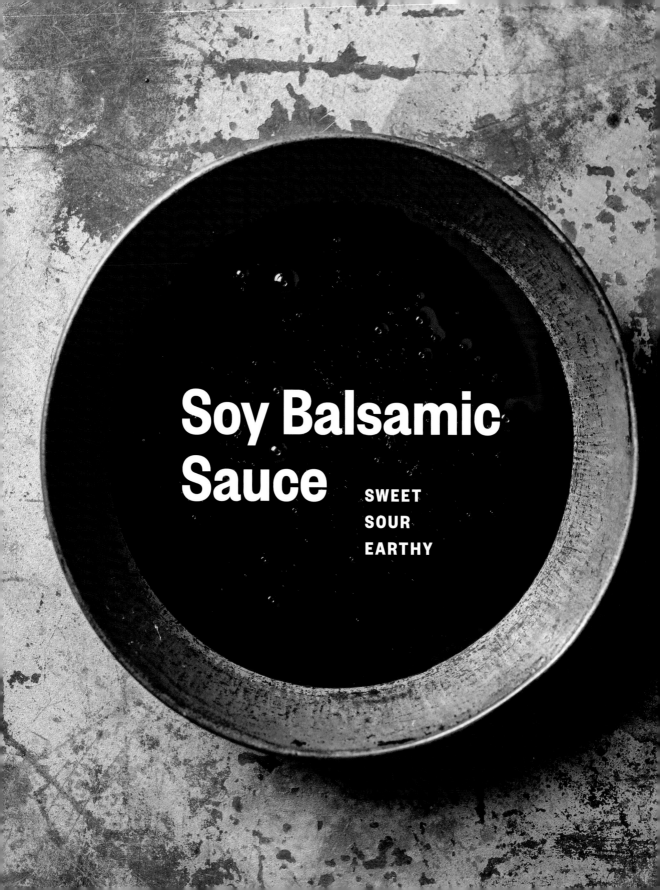

Soy Balsamic Sauce

SWEET

SOUR

EARTHY

This recipe is very dear to my heart, as it was my first attempt to use ingredients that didn't normally go together, but made sense to me. In Asian cooking, vinegar is often used to cut saltiness from soy sauce or other ingredients. For me, balsamic vinegar has the perfect mix of sweetness, acidity, and body to combine with the brown sugar and soy sauce here.

1 teaspoon cornstarch, or as needed
2 tablespoons water
¼ cup dark brown sugar, firmly packed
½ cup balsamic vinegar
½ cup soy sauce

PREP TIME 10 minutes
COOK TIME 10 minutes
MAKES 1 cup

—

In a small bowl, stir together the cornstarch and water until the cornstarch dissolves and the mixture is the consistency of heavy cream, adding more cornstarch if the mixture is too thin.

Combine the brown sugar, vinegar, and soy sauce in a small saucepan and bring to a boil over medium heat, stirring to dissolve the sugar. Stir the cornstarch mixture briefly to recombine, then stir it into the soy-vinegar mixture and simmer over low heat for about 3 minutes, until the sauce thickens enough to coat the back of a spoon.

Remove from the heat, let cool completely, then refrigerate in an airtight container. This sauce will last for months without going bad.

Soy Balsamic Sauce

Ko-Rican Sauce

TANGY

EARTHY

GARLICKY

Once I married a Puerto Rican woman, my food became what we call a little Ko-Rican, and that's what this sauce is all about. I learned this recipe from my mother-in-law, Dolores Alicea, aka Doe or Lola. Let me tell you, the best Puerto Rican restaurant in town is her house! When I tasted her turkey *lechon* at our first Thanksgiving together, it was all over for me. The bright flavors, the spiciness from the garlic, the tanginess from the vinegar—everything was new to me. From the moment I tasted her sauces, I knew I had to learn how to make them. I never put vinegar in my marinades until I met Lola, but I understood why cooks put alcohol in marinades, and this is similar: it tenderizes and accentuates the flavors. Now, her cooking is part of my DNA. I had to add it to my arsenal of kitchen techniques, but of course, I made a few changes to kung fu it.

2 tablespoons sweet paprika

2 tablespoons dried oregano

2 tablespoons chili powder

2 tablespoons Madras curry powder

¼ cup salt

½ cup distilled white vinegar

26 cloves garlic, minced

½ cup olive oil

PREP TIME 10 minutes
MAKES 1½ cups

—

Combine the paprika, oregano, chili powder, curry powder, salt, vinegar, garlic, and oil in a small bowl and whisk until well mixed. Transfer to an airtight container and refrigerate for up 2 weeks or freeze for up to 2 months (see note).

NOTE This sauce won't fully harden when frozen, so you can spoon out as much as you need whenever you want to use it.

Ko-Rican Sauce

Nuoc Cham Sauce

SALTY

GARLICKY

FUNKY

TANGY

I learned about *nuoc cham* from Arun Sampanthavivat, whose Chicago restaurant, Arun's, is considered to be one of the best Thai restaurants in the world. *Nuoc cham* is a Vietnamese dipping sauce with big, bright flavors; it's tangy, funky, sour, and sweet all at once. I add green Thai chilies to give it some heat and use it not only as a dipping sauce but also as the base for marinades and dressings. This sauce is also a great foundation for things you wouldn't consider very Asian, like my Korean pesto (page 46) and even my pimento cheese dip (page 66).

¼ cup dark brown sugar, firmly packed
¼ cup fresh lime juice
¼ cup fish sauce
½ cup water
1 clove garlic, minced
2 green Thai chilies, minced, with seeds

PREP TIME 10 minutes
MAKES 1 cup

——

Combine the brown sugar, lime juice, fish sauce, water, garlic, and chilies in a small bowl and whisk until the sugar dissolves. Transfer to an airtight container and refrigerate for up to 2 weeks or freeze for up to 2 months. Or freeze in standard ice-cube trays, then transfer the cubes (2 tablespoons each) to plastic freezer bags and freeze for up to 2 months.

Nuoc Cham Sauce

Magic Paste

SPICY
PEPPERY
ANISE

I call this Magic Paste because, for me, it's the ideal combination of ingredients. It's got sweet spiciness from the ginger, funkiness from the fish sauce, nuttiness from the sesame oil, and gentle heat from the Korean chili flakes. This paste is the secret to how we make kimchi every day at our restaurants.

1 (1-inch) piece fresh ginger, peeled and sliced

5 cloves garlic, peeled

2 tablespoons fennel seeds

½ cup fish sauce

¼ cup toasted sesame oil

¼ cup Korean chili flakes

PREP TIME 10 minutes
MAKES 1 cup

—

Combine the ginger, garlic, and fennel seeds in a food processor and process until minced, periodically scraping down the sides of the bowl to make sure all of the ginger gets chopped. Add the fish sauce, oil, and chili flakes and process for 30 seconds.

Transfer to an airtight container and refrigerate for up to 2 weeks or freeze for up to 2 months. Or freeze in standard ice-cube trays, then transfer the cubes (about 2 tablespoons each) to plastic freezer bags and freeze for up to 2 months.

Magic Paste

Korean Pesto

HERBAL
NUTTY
BRIGHT
SPICY

Okay, I know you're wondering what pesto has to do with Korean barbecue. But pesto doesn't have to be exclusive to Italian cooking. It's just a combination of nuts and oil and herbs and other ingredients, and it can be used in anything from a dipping sauce to a soup to a marinade. So I took Asian versions of these ingredients—like kimchi instead of cheese for a little fermented element—and created a similarly balanced sauce that is distinctly Korean. It adds intensity and will elevate the flavors in your food.

¼ cup Nuoc Cham Sauce (page 42)

¼ cup Lemongrass Chili Sauce (page 36)

1 chipotle chili in adobo sauce, plus 1 tablespoon adobo sauce

¼ cup kimchi, homemade (page 166) or store-bought

¼ cup dry-roasted peanuts

½ cup fresh basil leaves, firmly packed

¼ cup olive oil

PREP TIME 10 minutes
MAKES 1 cup

—

Place the Nuoc Cham Sauce, chili sauce, chipotle chili and adobo sauce, kimchi, peanuts, basil, and oil in a food processor and process for about 1 minute, until coarsely blended.

Transfer to an airtight container and refrigerate for up to 2 weeks or freeze for up to 2 months. Or freeze in standard ice-cube trays, then transfer the cubes (about 2 tablespoons each) to plastic freezer bags and freeze for up to 2 months.

Korean Pesto

Blackening Seasoning

PEPPERY

GARLICKY

SMOKY

When I was a kid, I used to watch Justin Wilson's *Cookin' Cajun* TV show after school; it came on right after the *Tom and Jerry* cartoons. I loved it when he'd lean into the camera and tell you, "Ou-wheeeee! I garontee you'll like this!" Watching those old shows still makes me laugh, but his food was serious. He cooked with rice and crayfish, so it kind of reminded me of the Korean food from home. In a way, he was my Julia Child. I'm still a huge fan of Cajun food, and I'll pick up a jar of hot pickled okra (which is kind of like kimchi) at the store and eat it in the car. I can't stop myself—sometimes I finish it before I even get home! As Justin would say, I garontee this seasoning will become part of your cooking!

¼ cup sweet paprika
¼ cup granulated garlic or garlic powder
¼ cup chili powder
2 teaspoons kosher salt

PREP TIME 5 minutes
MAKES ¾ cup

——

Combine the paprika, granulated garlic, chili powder, and salt in a small bowl and stir to mix. Store in an airtight container in a cool, dark cupboard for up to 6 months.

Blackening Seasoning

Curry
Salt

EARTHY

SPICY

SALTY

Plain salt is boring! I want more flavor when I season something. When I cooked in high-end French restaurants, I was taught to be restrained in my seasoning. But once I started making my own food, I realized that I didn't have to follow that rule, and I didn't have to use plain salt when I could make something with more flavor. This robustly flavored salt is an essential component of how we season food at our restaurants. It helps us build those subtle flavors that you can't quite identify but know are what make the food so tasty.

¼ cup Madras curry powder
¼ cup kosher salt
1 tablespoon shichimi togarashi

PREP TIME 5 minutes
MAKES ½ cup

—

Combine the curry powder, salt, and shichimi togarashi in a small bowl and stir to mix. Store in an airtight container in a cool, dark cupboard for up to 6 months.

Curry Salt

BBQ Spice Rub

SMOKY

SWEET

GARLICKY

Korean chili flakes give you the smoky, sweet flavors of chilies without all of the heat. In this rub, they are joined by brown sugar, which creates a memorable caramelized coating on whatever you grill.

¼ cup dark brown sugar, firmly packed
¼ cup Blackening Seasoning (page 48)
2 teaspoons ground black pepper
¼ cup Korean chili flakes
2 tablespoons kosher salt

PREP TIME 5 minutes
MAKES 1 cup

––

Combine the brown sugar, Blackening Seasoning, pepper, chili flakes, and salt in a small bowl and stir to mix. Store in an airtight container in a cool, dark cupboard for up to 6 months.

USE THIS TO MAKE

BBQ Spice Rub

Snacks and Drinks

As soon as you order at a traditional Korean barbecue restaurant, your table is filled with *banchan*, dozens of little snacks and sides to go along with the grilled meats. When you are barbecuing at home, it's just as important to have a lot of snacks to munch on while the grill heats up and you're hanging out with your friends. No one wants the guests standing around staring at their phones until the fire is ready. Give them something to do, something interesting and tasty to eat and drink and talk about, and your barbecue is already off to a good start.

The best snacks are ones that you can make in advance, can be eaten cold or at room temperature, have a lot flavor, and will get everyone's appetite fired up. But while they should keep hunger at bay so no one is starving, they shouldn't be "dinner killers" that leave everyone too full to enjoy everything you're grilling. These recipes are some of my favorites for getting a meal started at our restaurants and at home. I especially like experimenting with new types of spreads and small bites, becuase people always seem willing to try a little snack they've never had before. Sipping a cocktail, snacking on spiced nuts or a totally new kind of hummus, talking with your friends—that's how the best parties get going.

Garlic Herb Peanuts

You might as well make a double batch of these spicy nuts, because I don't know anyone who doesn't eat handful after handful while enjoying a drink. The flavors of the toasted garlic, rosemary, and the *togarashi* in the Curry Salt come together in a way that's pretty irresistible. It's important to use dry-roasted peanuts for this recipe, because you are going to toss them in oil.

—

¼ cup olive oil

4 cloves garlic, thinly sliced

2 rosemary sprigs

2 cups dry-roasted peanuts

1 tablespoon Curry Salt (page 50)

2 teaspoons Korean chili flakes

PREP TIME 4 minutes
COOK TIME 25 minutes
FEEDS 6 people

Heat the oil in a sauté pan over medium-high heat for 2 minutes. Add the garlic and cook, stirring occasionally, for about 1 minute, until golden but not dark brown. Using a slotted spoon, remove the garlic slices from the pan and drain them on paper towels.

Carefully place the rosemary sprigs in the same pan (step back from the stove as you add them in case the oil splatters). Cook for about 1 minute, until the leaves turn brittle in the hot oil. Turn off the heat, remove the sprigs from the pan, and drain them on paper towels. Let the rosemary sit until cool enough to handle, then strip the leaves from the stems and chop the leaves finely. Let the flavored olive oil cool for 20 minutes.

Transfer the peanuts to a bowl, spoon 1 tablespoon of the cooled oil over the peanuts, and toss to coat evenly. Add the Curry Salt, chili flakes, garlic slices, and rosemary leaves, toss well again, and serve.

KUNG FU IT Don't toss out the extra flavored oil—it's gold! Save it to cook other dishes; I like to use it for sautéing chicken or pork.

Clockwise from top:
Garlic Herb Peanuts,
Grilled Shishito Peppers
(page 70), and Edamame
Hummus (page 61).

Hoisin and Yuzu Edamame

I like to keep bags of edamame in the freezer. They are perfect for a quick, healthy snack and require almost no time or effort to cook. If you have Soy Balsamic Sauce in your fridge and edamame in the freezer, this snack comes together in just minutes.

———

6 cups water

1 (1-pound) bag frozen edamame in the pod

¾ cup Soy Balsamic Sauce (page 38)

2 tablespoons hoisin sauce

1 tablespoon bottled yuzu juice or fresh lime or lemon juice

1 tablespoon Korean chili flakes

Bring the water to a boil in a large saucepan over high heat. Add the edamame and cook for about 4 minutes, until tender. Meanwhile, set up a large bowl of ice water. When the edamame are ready, drain them and immediately immerse them in the ice water to halt the cooking.

Whisk together the Soy Balsamic Sauce, hoisin sauce, yuzu juice, and chili flakes in a large bowl. Drain the edamame well, add them to the sauce, stir to combine, and serve.

PREP TIME 15 minutes
COOK TIME 10 minutes
FEEDS 6 people

Korean BBQ

Edamame Hummus

I eat hummus every day—no lie. Sometimes I even eat it for breakfast, with tuna salad, avocado, and rice crackers; that's how much I like it. So I'm always thinking about ways to make new hummus recipes with something other than chickpeas. This one lightens up traditional hummus by replacing the chickpeas with edamame, citrus, and avocado (pictured on page 58). Serve it with cut-up vegetables, rice crackers, or tortilla chips.

—

4 cups water, plus up to ⅔ cup for thinning

2 cups frozen shelled edamame

■ 2 tablespoons Curry Salt (page 50)

■ 1 teaspoon BBQ Spice Rub (page 52)

1 ripe avocado, halved, pitted, peeled, and cut into chunks

1 tablespoon extra-hot prepared horseradish

1 tablespoon Dijon mustard

¼ cup fresh lemon juice

1 tablespoon sambal oelek

10 basil leaves, thinly sliced

PREP TIME 20 minutes
COOK TIME 8 minutes
FEEDS 6 people

Bring the 4 cups water to boil in a medium saucepan over high heat. Add the edamame and cook for about 4 minutes, until tender. Meanwhile, set up a large bowl of ice water. When the edamame are ready, drain them and immediately immerse them in the ice water to halt the cooking. Let the edamame sit in the ice water until cold, then drain.

Place the edamame, Curry Salt, spice rub, avocado, horseradish, mustard, lemon juice, sambal oelek, and basil in a food processor and process for about 2 minutes, until smooth. Add water as needed (up to ⅔ cup) to thin to the desired consistency. Transfer to a bowl and serve.

KUNG FU IT You should eat this hummus within a day of making it because the avocado will oxidize (and turn brown), but if you need to save it overnight, I have a great tip for you that will lessen the browning. Put the hummus in an airtight container, then place a sheet of plastic wrap directly on the surface of the hummus, pressing it down gently so no air is trapped between the plastic wrap and the hummus. Put the lid on the container and refrigerate it.

Spicy Crab Dip

I really enjoy having dips and chips at parties, but too often those dips contain dairy, which I'm allergic to. So this is the dip I created for my own selfish reasons. Tofu cream cheese is the perfect replacement for regular cream cheese in recipes like this one, as it adds a silkiness and creaminess reminiscent of the regular version with dairy. Eat this dip with something crunchy, like celery, radishes, or even rice cakes.

—

- 2 tablespoons Nuoc Cham Sauce (page 42)
- ½ cup tofu cream cheese
- 6 cilantro sprigs, chopped, with stems
- 2 green onions, white and green parts, thinly sliced
- 1 teaspoon fish sauce
- 1 tablespoon sambal oelek
- 1 teaspoon Korean chili flakes
- 2 teaspoons fresh lemon juice
- 8 ounces crabmeat, picked over for shell fragments (see note)

PREP TIME 20 minutes
FEEDS 6 people

Place the Nuoc Cham Sauce, tofu cream cheese, cilantro, green onions, fish sauce, sambal oelek, chili flakes, and lemon juice in a food processor and process for about 1 minute, until smooth. Scrape the mixture into a bowl, gently fold in the crab, and serve.

NOTE I like to use jumbo lump crabmeat from blue crabs for this dip. If you are on the East Coast, you can use Jonah crabmeat, and on the West Coast, look for Dungeness crabmeat.

Korean Baba Ghanoush

My mom always cooked eggplant, and growing up I saw her grill, roast, and fry it all the time. Then one day when I was about ten years old, I watched her steam the eggplant until it was mush, which puzzled me. She told me to be patient, then she added sesame oil, garlic, green onions, chili flakes, and soy sauce, and made this delicious eggplant snack that I still remember (and make) today. I cook my eggplant on the grill to add a little smokiness to this Korean version of baba ghanoush, and add black beans because they give the dip a creamy texture. Serve this with rice crackers, tortilla chips, or my favorite, radishes.

—

4 Chinese eggplants, halved lengthwise

4 tablespoons olive oil

■ 1 teaspoon Curry Salt (page 50)

■ ½ cup Nuoc Cham Sauce (page 42)

1 tablespoon toasted sesame oil

1 tablespoon sambal oelek

1 (15-ounce) can black beans, drained

1 teaspoon chili powder

1 teaspoon Korean chili flakes

¼ cup chopped fresh cilantro

PREP TIME 20 minutes
COOK TIME 16 minutes
FEEDS 6 people

Heat the grill for direct heat cooking to medium (350°F to 375°F).

Brush the eggplant halves with 2 tablespoons of the olive oil and sprinkle the Curry Salt on top. Place the eggplants on the grill, close the lid, and cook for 4 minutes. Flip the eggplants over, close the lid, and cook for another 4 minutes. Cook, flip, and cook the eggplants one more time for about 4 minutes on each side, until lightly charred on both sides and tender. Remove from the grill and let cool for 10 minutes.

Coarsely chop the eggplants and transfer to a food processor. Add the remaining 2 tablespoons olive oil, the Nuoc Cham Sauce, sesame oil, sambal oelek, black beans, chili powder, chili flakes, and cilantro and process for about 2 minutes, until smooth. Transfer to a bowl and serve.

KUNG FU IT This baba ghanoush can be made a couple of days in advance and kept in the refrigerator. It also makes a good sandwich spread or a sauce to accompany grilled or roasted meat.

Seoulthern Pimento Cheese

In the early 1990s, I lived in Atlanta for a year while working as a cook, and that's when I was introduced to pimento cheese. At first, I really didn't know what it was. A cheese ball? A dip? Was it supposed to be served hot or cold? I was so confused! Then I asked a local what to do with it, and he told me to use it as a spread on a sandwich or on a cracker—or just to eat it right out of the jar. Once I tried it, I immediately fell in love with it. Dips like this are a great snack at a barbecue with rice cakes, crackers, grilled bread, or raw celery.

---

1 cup shredded sharp Cheddar cheese

½ cup tofu cream cheese

¼ cup mayonnaise

3 tablespoons Nuoc Cham Sauce (page 42)

¼ cup jarred diced pimentos

2 green onions, white and green parts, thinly sliced

2 teaspoons ground black pepper

1 teaspoon onion powder

1 teaspoon garlic powder

2 teaspoons sambal oelek

2 teaspoons Korean chili flakes

PREP TIME 10 minutes
FEEDS 6 people

In a stand mixer fitted with the paddle attachment, combine the Cheddar cheese, tofu cream cheese, mayonnaise, Nuoc Cham Sauce, pimentos, green onions, black pepper, onion powder, garlic powder, sambal oelek, and chili flakes and beat on medium speed until thoroughly mixed. You can instead combine all of the ingredients in a food processor and process for about 30 seconds. Transfer to a bowl and serve.

Toasted Sesame Gim Bites

In our family, the first solid food a newborn gets to eat is *gim* with steamed rice. *Gim* is the Korean word for nori, which are sheets of dried seaweed. When I get a craving for *gim*, I go to a local Korean market and get myself a treat for the road, usually Korean blood sausage, toasted *gim* snacks, and a peeled grape drink. It's one of the little things in life that I really enjoy.

—

1 tablespoon vegetable oil

1 teaspoon toasted sesame oil

6 nori (gim) sheets, each about 8 inches square

½ teaspoon kosher salt

■ 1 teaspoon BBQ Spice Rub (page 52)

PREP TIME 2 minutes
COOK TIME 2 minutes
FEEDS 6 people

Heat the grill for direct heat grilling to medium (350°F to 375°F).

Mix together the vegetable oil and sesame oil in a small bowl. Arrange the nori sheets in a single layer on a cutting board, brush each one on both sides with the oil mixture, and then lightly season on both sides with the salt.

In batches, place the nori sheets on the grill, press them onto the grate with a spatula, and cook for about 20 seconds, until they turn green. Flip the sheets over and cook for another 20 seconds. Return the sheets to the cutting board and sprinkle them on both sides with the spice rub. Cut the sheets into quarters and serve.

KUNG FU IT When I was a kid, I used to toast *gim* sheets in the toaster. If you do the same, brush them with oil after toasting instead of before, and keep an eye on them, as they'll burn easily in a toaster. You can store the toasted sheets in an airtight container at room temperature for up to a week.

Grilled Shishito Peppers with Korean Pesto

Brent, Beth, Ellie, and Ava Eccles from Green Acres Farm in Indiana are friends of mine and part of our restaurant family. They grow the best shishito peppers in the country, hands down. All year I look forward to these peppers coming into season and showing up at the Chicago Green City Market. Most shishito peppers are very mild, but you have to always be on alert: one out of every ten is surprisingly spicy. For some reason, I always get a spicy one!

—

2 pounds shishito peppers

¼ cup olive oil

1 tablespoon Curry Salt (page 50)

1½ cups Korean Pesto (page 46)

PREP TIME 5 minutes
COOK TIME 6 minutes
FEEDS 6 people

Heat the grill for direct heat cooking to medium (350°F to 375°F).

Place the peppers in a large bowl, drizzle with the oil, and toss the peppers to coat evenly. Season the peppers with the Curry Salt and toss again.

Place the peppers on the grill, close the lid, and cook, turning once, for about 3 minutes on each side, until blistered and blackened in spots. Serve the peppers immediately with the pesto as a dipping sauce.

Kiwi Mint Sake Cocktail

This cocktail was inspired by a trip I took to Brazil in 2005. Every time I make this drink, it takes me back to that visit and to my memories of Brazilian culture, of how much people there enjoy life, and of my surprise at all the strong Japanese influences. If I'm asked to bring a cocktail to a party or a dinner, this is my go-to recipe. It has a nice balance of tart and sweet flavors and is super refreshing on a hot day.

—

2 cups coarsely chopped, peeled kiwi

3 limes, sliced and seeded

2 lemons, sliced and seeded

¼ cup sugar

4 mint sprigs, plus 6 small sprigs for garnish

2 cups sparkling water, chilled

2 cups sake, chilled

Ice, for serving

Place the kiwi, limes, lemons, sugar, and mint in a large pitcher and muddle them together with a large wooden spoon, pressing down to release the fruit juices. Stir in the sparkling water and sake. Pour into glasses over ice and garnish with the mint sprigs.

PREP TIME 20 minutes
SERVES 6 people

Snacks and Drinks

Lychee Drinking Vinegar

In Korea, fruit vinegar shots are very popular. They are becoming popular in America, too, with fruit vinegar shrubs (a mixture of fruit, sugar, and vinegar) being used more and more in cocktails. I can't do straight vinegar shots, but I'm a huge fan of drinking vinegar cocktails. I use a young coconut vinegar, which has the same amount of acid as lime or lemon juice, so you can swap in one of those if you prefer. But it is worth your time to look for coconut vinegar. It gives the drink a mild, tropical sweet-tart flavor that makes it pretty special.

———

¾ cup coconut vinegar (I prefer Silver Swan brand)

34 drained canned lychees, liquid reserved

⅓ cup lychee juice from canned lychees

¾ cup sugar

½ cup water

Pinch of kosher salt

24 mint sprigs

8 lemon slices

6 cups sparkling water, chilled

8 vodka shots, chilled (optional)

4 cups ice

To make the cocktail base, combine the vinegar, 10 of the lychees, the lychee juice, sugar, water, and salt in a blender and blend for 1 minute, until smooth.

Pour the cocktail base into a large pitcher, add the mint, the remaining 24 lychees, and the lemon slices, and muddle with a large wooden spoon for about 30 seconds, pressing down to release the fruit juices. Add the sparkling water and vodka, stir well, add the ice, and then serve.

PREP TIME 10 minutes
SERVES 8 people

Thai Basil Lemonade

Tang was my favorite thing to drink when I was very young and there was always a pitcher of it somewhere in our refrigerator. I have moved up in the world since then, but I still love a citrusy drink. My beverage of choice nowadays is lemonade with herbs, usually mint or basil (pictured on page 76, in center). The twist here is the Thai basil, which gives the drink a floral note and a hint of anise flavor. It makes a light drink that is easy to sip all day long.

—

1 cup sugar

½ cup fresh Thai basil or regular basil leaves, loosely packed

2 large lemons, halved and seeded

8 cups water

1 cup fresh lemon juice

4 cups ice

PREP TIME 5 minutes
SERVES 6 people

Place the sugar, basil, and lemons in a large pitcher and muddle with a large wooden spoon until very fragrant. Add the water, lemon juice, and ice, stir well to dissolve the sugar, and serve.

KUNG FU IT I like to make a drink of half Thai Basil Lemonade and half Iced Green Hornet (page 76). It's like a Korean Arnold Palmer.

Iced Green Hornet

This is my power drink, which I down every day right before our restaurants open (pictured below, at right). It's a serious miracle worker, giving you real energy without the crash you get an hour later from sugary drinks. You can make a batch of it to drink over the course of a few days, but be sure to stir it well before pouring it, as the *matcha* will settle to the bottom.

—

6 tablespoons sugar

2 tablespoons matcha
(green tea powder)

6 cups water

6 cups ice

6 mint sprigs

6 lime slices

Combine the sugar and matcha in a bowl and stir to mix well. Very slowly add the water while whisking vigorously to prevent lumps from forming. Transfer to a pitcher.

Divide the ice among 6 glasses and add a mint sprig to each glass. Pour in the tea and garnish each serving with a lime slice.

PREP TIME 5 minutes
SERVES 6 people

Vietnamese Iced Coffee

Vietnamese coffee has a strong coffee flavor that I really enjoy, and it's at its best when you use this cold brew method. You get the pure taste of coffee, plus it is especially easy to make: just let it steep overnight and your iced coffee is nearly ready to go the next morning.

—

2 cups medium-coarse ground dark roast coffee (I prefer Café Du Monde)

8 cups water

¾ cup sweetened condensed milk

Ice, for serving

PREP TIME 5 minutes
STEEP TIME 12 hours
SERVES 6 people

Combine the ground coffee and water in a large container with a lid. Stir gently but thoroughly with a wooden spoon, then cover and let steep overnight in the refrigerator. The next day, line a strainer with cheesecloth or a coffee filter and pour the coffee through the strainer into a clean container.

You should have about 6 cups coffee. Whisk in the condensed milk, then cover tightly and refrigerate for up to a week. Pour over ice to serve.

NOTE This recipe serves 6, but you can also keep the strained steeped coffee in the refrigerator for up to 2 weeks. Then, when you want a single cup to start the day, whisk together 1 cup of the cold brew and 3 tablespoons condensed milk and pour over ice.

Snacks and Drinks

BBQ Meats

The smell of meat barbecuing is everywhere in Seoul. When you walk down a side street, you'll see a canopy of tents off to the side. These are street-food stalls, and when you enter one, you are welcomed and then instructed to sit on a stool in front of a large steel drum filled with burning coal. The grate on top is where you'll cook your meat and is also your table (just don't put your elbows on this table!). The cook will bring over a tray laden with lettuce cups, dipping sauces, and chili pastes, and a platter of thinly sliced meats in marinade. You'll use your chopsticks or mini tongs to grill the meats and then you'll eat them as they are ready. It is pure Korean barbecue—no fuss.

It's obviously different in America, but grilling at the park was one of my favorite family outings when I was a kid. We would head to the Forest Preserves, which are huge nature parks in Chicago, with friends and family. We'd get the grills going, and then my mom would pull out the meat that she had marinated for hours and place it on the grill. Sometimes strangers would pass by, smell the tangy marinated meats cooking on the grill, and wander over to ask what we were making. Mom, who was a Korean barbecue evangelist from the beginning, would always give them a sample to try. It was probably their first bite of Korean barbecue and the first time they met and talked to a Korean person, and the smiles on their faces once they bit into the food revealed how much they liked it.

Koreans don't traditionally grill at home much, but that's changed for Koreans in America. We usually use thin cuts of meat instead of the giant steaks and hot dogs you see on most American grills, but the essence of getting together with family and friends to eat, relax, and have fun is the same.

Korean BBQ Skirt Steak

This recipe calls for skirt steak, which has a ton of flavor and cooks quickly. Get the inside skirt steak (which comes from the flank) if you can; it's thinner and cooks faster than the outside skirt steak (which is from between the brisket and flank). The Korean BBQ Sauce marinade is similar to what my mother made to marinate meats for grilling when I was a kid. I really enjoy eating steak this way; the crisp lettuce and herbs help cut the richness of the meat.

---

3 pounds skirt steak

■ 2 cups Korean BBQ Sauce (page 34)

■ 2 cups Korean Pesto (page 46)

12 Bibb lettuce leaves

¼ cup fresh basil and cilantro leaves, loosely packed

PREP TIME 10 minutes
MARINATE TIME 1 to 12 hours
COOK TIME 4 minutes
FEEDS 6 people

Place the steak in a large, shallow dish, pour the BBQ sauce over the steak, and turn the steak to coat evenly. Cover and marinate in the refrigerator for at least 1 hour or preferably overnight.

Heat the grill for direct heat cooking to medium-high (400°F to 450°F).

Place the steak on the grill grate and cook, turning once, for about 2 minutes on each side, until lightly charred. Transfer the steak to a cutting board and let rest for 5 minutes.

Thinly slice the meat against the grain and serve with the pesto, lettuce cups, and herbs.

NOTE It's important to cut the skirt steak the correct way. Otherwise, the meat will be too tough to eat. Look at the steak to see the direction the muscle fibers are running. That's the grain. You want to slice it thinly against the grain.

Ko-Rican Pork Chops

I like to say my food is Ko-Rican—half Korean, half Puerto Rican—the perfect balance of Zen and *fuego*. You can taste it in how the Ko-Rican Sauce is used in this recipe, as a marinade for the pork and as the basis for a punchy, bright, acidic Korean *chimichurri*. I was raised on inexpensive variety packs of pork chops, which contain razor-thin slices of meat on the bone. It blew my mind when I learned that pork chops come in different thicknesses and sizes. I still like my thin pork chops, however, as they are easy to cook and marinate in no time. If you can't find thin pork chops, add a couple of minutes to the grilling time on each side.

---

6 (½-pound) bone-in pork chops, ¼ inch thick

■ 2¼ cups Ko-Rican Sauce (page 40)

■ ¼ cup Nuoc Cham Sauce (page 42)

¼ cup coarsely chopped fresh flat-leaf parsley

¼ cup coarsely chopped fresh cilantro

1 tablespoon sambal oelek

PREP TIME 10 minutes
MARINATE TIME 20 minutes to 12 hours
COOK TIME 6 minutes
FEEDS 6 people

Place the pork chops in a large, shallow dish, pour 2 cups of the Ko-Rican Sauce over the chops, and turn the chops to coat evenly. Cover and marinate at room temperature for 20 minutes or preferably in the refrigerator for at least 4 hours or up to overnight.

While the pork is marinating, make the Korean *chimichurri*. Combine the Nuoc Cham Sauce, remaining ¼ cup Ko-Rican Sauce, parsley, cilantro, and sambal oelek in a food processor and process for about 1 minute, until smooth. Set aside at room temperature.

Heat the grill for direct heat cooking to medium-high (400°F to 450°F).

Remove the chops from the marinade and shake off the excess marinade. Place them on the grill and cook, turning them once, for 2 to 3 minutes on each side, until lightly charred. Remove the chops from the grill and let rest for 5 minutes, then serve with the *chimichurri*.

Slow-Grilled Ko-Rican-Style Baby Back Ribs

The key to cooking these ribs on a grill is to do it low and slow. That means over indirect heat so the ribs are next to, rather than directly over, the fire and the lid is closed. This method turns the grill into an outdoor oven, and the ribs don't burn on the outside before turning soft and tender on the inside. I always want to grab one of these straight off the grill, but you'll burn yourself on the hot bones if you don't wait for a few minutes—trust me on that!

—

■ 1½ cups Ko-Rican Sauce (page 40)

▪ 1½ cups Lemongrass Chili Sauce (page 36)

2 tablespoons ground black pepper

3 racks baby back pork ribs

PREP TIME 15 minutes
MARINATE TIME 30 minutes
COOK TIME 2½ hours
FEEDS 6 people

Combine the Ko-Rican Sauce, chili sauce, and pepper in a large, shallow dish and mix well. Add the ribs and turn to coat evenly. Marinate at room temperature for 30 minutes.

Heat the grill for indirect heat cooking to medium-low (300°F to 325°F). (If using a charcoal grill, rake the coals to one side of the charcoal grate; if using a gas grill, turn off half of the burners.)

While the grill is heating, lay a large sheet of heavy-duty aluminum foil on a work surface. Remove a rack of ribs from the marinade, place in the center of the foil, and then spoon some of the marinade onto the ribs. Bring the sides of the foil together, wrapping the ribs tightly and securing the seams closed. Place the packet on a second large sheet of foil and wrap the packet in the foil, sealing the edges and corners securely to make sure no liquid will escape. Repeat the process with the remaining racks.

Place the ribs in an ovenproof skillet or even in the grill's drip pan, then place the pan on the grill grate away from direct heat. Close the lid and cook the ribs for 2 hours. If using a charcoal grill, add hot coals to the fire as needed to maintain the temperature.

Remove the foil-wrapped ribs from the grill and let the packet rest for about 10 minutes. Then unwrap the package, saving the foil and all of the juices collected in it. Work carefully, as the ribs will be very hot and tender and they can break apart.

CONTINUED

Slow-Grilled Ko-Rican-Style Baby Back Ribs

CONTINUED

Increase the heat of the grill to medium-high (400°F to 450°F). Place the ribs, meat side down, directly on the grate over the fire and cook for 5 minutes. Flip the ribs over and cook for 2 to 4 minutes on the other side, until they have a little char. Transfer the ribs to a cutting board and let rest for 15 minutes.

Cut the ribs apart and arrange them on one or more serving platters. Spoon the juices from the foil packet over the ribs and serve.

KUNG FU IT If you don't have time to cook the ribs fully on the grill (or want to get a head start), you can cook them in a 300°F oven for 2 hours, then finish them on the grill to caramelize the exterior and capture all that flavor from the fire.

Korean al Pastor

This recipe is for Rafa, our head prep cook at bellyQ, who always asks me if we can open a taqueria together on a beach one day. If we ever pull it off, this would be one of our opening recipes. Just thinking about the tropical flavors of the pineapple juice, cilantro, and grilled pineapple makes my mouth water.

—

- 1 cup Ko-Rican Sauce (page 40)
  ½ cup gochujang
  ½ cup pineapple juice
  1 yellow onion, finely chopped
  ¼ cup honey
  3 pounds boneless pork shoulder, cut against the grain into ¼-inch-thick slices
  1 pineapple, peeled, cut into ½-inch-wide rings, and rings cored
  ½ cup loosely packed fresh cilantro leaves, finely chopped
  Kosher salt
  Corn tortillas, warmed, for serving
  Lettuce cups, for serving
  Sliced yellow onions, for serving

PREP TIME 15 minutes
MARINATE TIME 1 hour
COOK TIME 10 minutes
FEEDS 6 to 8 people

Combine the Ko-Rican Sauce, gochujang, pineapple juice, chopped yellow onion, and honey in a large, shallow dish and mix well. Add the pork slices and turn to coat evenly. Cover and marinate in the refrigerator for 1 hour.

Heat the grill for direct heat cooking to medium-high (400°F to 450°F).

Place the pineapple slices on the grill grate and cook, turning once, for 2 minutes on each side, until lightly charred. Transfer the pineapple to a cutting board, let cool until it can be handled, then finely chop. Combine the pineapple and cilantro in a bowl, toss to combine, and set aside until ready to use.

While the pineapple is cooling, place the pork slices on the grill grate, season with salt, and cook, turning once, for about 3 minutes on each side, until lightly charred. Transfer the pork to a serving platter and let it rest for 3 minutes. While the pork is resting, place the corn tortillas on the grill to warm them slightly on each side before serving.

Top the pork with the pineapple-cilantro salsa and serve with the tortillas, lettuce cups, and sliced yellow onions on the side.

Drunken BBQ Lamb Chops

My family never ate lamb when I was growing up, so I didn't try it until I got to culinary school. I quickly fell in love with it—chops, leg of lamb, and, of course, homemade gyros, which I still crave every now and again. Three ingredients in the marinade make this recipe special: the rosemary, hoisin sauce, and brandy. Rosemary is a classic seasoning for lamb, while the hoisin adds depth of flavor, the brandy lends a slight sweetness, and the alcohol accelerates the marinating process.

—

- ½ cup Soy Balsamic Sauce (page 38)
- ½ cup brandy
- ¼ cup hoisin sauce
- ¼ cup toasted sesame oil
- ¼ cup loosely packed fresh rosemary leaves, chopped
- 12 small cloves garlic, minced
- 16 lamb loin chops, about 1 inch thick

PREP TIME 15 minutes
MARINATE TIME 1 hour
COOK TIME 6 minutes
FEEDS 4 people

Combine the Soy Balsamic Sauce, brandy, hoisin sauce, sesame oil, rosemary, and garlic in a small bowl and mix well. Measure out one-fourth of the marinade and reserve it for basting the meat on the grill.

Place the lamb chops in a large, shallow dish. Spoon the remaining marinade over the chops and turn the chops to coat evenly. Marinate at room temperature for 1 hour.

Heat the grill for direct heat cooking to medium (350°F to 375°F).

Place the chops on the grill over the flames and cook for 3 minutes. Brush or lightly spoon some of the reserved marinade on the chops, turn the chops over, and brush or lightly spoon marinade on the second side. Cook the chops for about 3 minutes longer, until lightly charred on each side.

Transfer the chops to a serving platter and let rest for 4 minutes, then serve.

KUNG FU IT If you can't find lamb, this marinade also works well with the rich flavor of beef, so use it on steaks.

Mama Kim's Burgers

My mom didn't know what meat was used in hamburgers when we moved to America, so she took her dumpling filling and made it into burger patties. It was serious genius for her to blend Korean and American cultures, and I always tell her that if she did that in a food truck today, she'd be rich! I like to use a mix of ground short rib, chuck, and skirt steak for the meat and potato buns for the buns.

—

5 napa cabbage leaves

1 tablespoon Curry Salt (page 50)

½ cup Lemongrass Chili Sauce (page 36)

½ cup finely chopped fresh cilantro

3 pounds ground beef (85 percent lean)

Kosher salt

6 hamburger buns, split

PREP TIME 30 minutes
COOK TIME 6 to 8 minutes
FEEDS 6 people

Heat the grill for direct heat cooking to medium (400°F to 450°F).

Stack the cabbage leaves, cut them crosswise into narrow strips, then chop the strips crosswise to create small squares. Transfer the cabbage to a large bowl, sprinkle with the Curry Salt, and mix well. (You want to make sure the Curry Salt is evenly distributed among the cabbage pieces and not in clumps.) Add the chili sauce, cilantro, and beef and mix gently until combined.

Divide the beef mixture into 6 equal portions (each about 8 ounces) and shape each portion into a patty ⅓ inch thick. Season the patties on both sides with kosher salt.

Place the patties on the grill grate and cook, turning them once, for 3 to 4 minutes on each side for medium, or until done to your liking. They should be lightly charred on both sides. Remove the burgers from the grill, then immediately place the buns, cut side down, on the grill grate for about 30 seconds, until lightly toasted.

Serve the burgers on the buns with your favorite condiments.

KUNG FU IT I like to mix together some Lemongrass Chili Sauce, hot sauce, and mayonnaise for a Korean secret sauce that takes these burgers to the next level.

Honey Soy Flank Steak

This is one amazing steak. It's simple to prepare and you get maximum flavor in a short period of time. Flank steak is a lean cut, so be careful you don't overcook it; medium-rare is ideal. Piercing the steak with a fork before marinating it is key to getting all of the rich, tangy, sweet flavors of the marinade throughout the meat.

—

1 cup Soy Balsamic Sauce (page 38)

⅓ cup vegetable oil

¼ cup honey

3 tablespoons distilled white vinegar

1 tablespoon kosher salt

2 teaspoons chili powder

3 pounds flank steak

PREP TIME 15 minutes
MARINATE TIME 1 hour
COOK TIME 8 minutes
FEEDS 6 people

Combine the Soy Balsamic Sauce, oil, honey, vinegar, salt, and chili powder in a bowl and whisk until well mixed. Place the flank steak in a large, shallow dish and pierce it all over with a fork. Pour the marinade over the steak and turn the steak to coat evenly. Cover and marinate at room temperature for 1 hour.

Heat the grill for direct heat cooking to medium (350° to 375°F).

Place the steak on the grill grate and cook, turning it once, for 3 to 4 minutes on each side for medium-rare. You can cook it a minute or two longer if you prefer your steak cooked medium, but flank steak should not be cooked past medium or it will be chewy.

Transfer the steak to a cutting board and let rest for 5 minutes. Thinly slice the steak against the grain, arrange the slices on a serving platter, and serve.

Jerk Pork Tenderloin Kebabs

Every winter, my wife, Yvonne, and I escape Chicago's snow and ice and head for a beach, a trip I always look forward to. One year we went to Jamaica, and I fell in love with the country and its food. I'm fascinated by jerk cooking and the deep flavors you get when you marinate the pork in soy, citrus, and spices and cook it over smoky wood. With this recipe, you get that jerk flavor Kung Fu–style, with bacon, kimchi, and spicy, juicy pork.

■ 1 cup Nuoc Cham Sauce (page 42)

½ cup kimchi, homemade (page 166) or store-bought

⅓ cup sambal oelek

¼ cup toasted sesame oil

2 tablespoons dark brown sugar

1 tablespoon fresh thyme leaves, or 1 teaspoon dried thyme

1 tablespoon fresh marjoram leaves, or 1 teaspoon dried marjoram

■ 1 tablespoon Curry Salt (page 50)

1 teaspoon ground allspice

½ teaspoon ground black pepper

¼ teaspoon ground cinnamon

3 pounds trimmed pork tenderloin, cut into 1-inch cubes

8 slices bacon

PREP TIME 30 minutes
MARINATE TIME 45 minutes
COOK TIME 8 minutes
FEEDS 4 people

You will need 8 skewers, either wooden or metal, each 8 inches long. If you are using wooden skewers, soak them in water for at least 30 minutes or until you are ready to use them.

Place the Nuoc Cham Sauce, kimchi, sambal oelek, oil, brown sugar, thyme, marjoram, Curry Salt, allspice, pepper, and cinnamon in a food processor and process for about 1 minute, until smooth. Measure out ½ cup of the marinade and reserve it for basting the meat on the grill.

Place the pork in a large, shallow dish, spoon the remaining marinade over the pork, and stir to coat evenly. Cover and marinate at room temperature for 45 minutes. While the pork is marinating, cut each bacon strip into 8 squares.

Heat the grill for direct heat cooking to medium (400°F to 450°F).

To load each skewer, thread on a cube of pork, follow it with 2 squares of bacon, and then repeat the order three more times and end with a pork cube. You should have a pork cube at the bottom and top of each skewer.

Place the skewers on the grill grate and cook for 4 minutes. Flip the kebabs over, brush with the reserved marinade, and cook for another 4 minutes, until lightly charred.

Transfer the kebabs to a serving platter and let rest for 4 minutes, then serve.

BBQ Meats

Tandoori Soy-Cumin Lamb

You might not think Indian and Korean food have a lot in common, but one afternoon while working on this book, my coauthor, Chandra, and I started talking about the similarities between the Indian food she grew up eating and the Korean food of my childhood. That conversation inspired me to create this recipe, so this is for you, Chandra! Indian cooks use yogurt to tenderize meat, and it plays that role here. I combine it with my Korean BBQ Sauce in a marinade that is a true culinary marriage of two Asian countries. I like to serve this lamb with pita bread, salad greens, and sliced onions.

—

- 1 cup Korean BBQ Sauce (page 34)
- ¾ cup Nuoc Cham Sauce (page 42)
- 2 cups plain Greek yogurt
- 1 tablespoon Curry Salt (page 50)
- 2½ tablespoons cumin seeds
- 1 (3-pound) boneless leg of lamb, butterflied or cut against the grain into ¼-inch-thick slices

PREP TIME 20 minutes
MARINATE TIME 3 hours
COOK TIME 4 to 24 minutes
FEEDS 6 people

Place the BBQ Sauce, Nuoc Cham Sauce, yogurt, Curry Salt, and cumin in a food processor and process for about 1 minute, until smooth. Measure out 1 cup of the marinade and reserve it for basting the meat on the grill.

Place the lamb in a large, shallow baking dish, spoon the remaining marinade over the lamb, and turn the lamb to coat evenly. Cover and marinate in the refrigerator for 3 hours.

Heat the grill for direct heat cooking to medium (350°F to 375°F).

Remove the lamb from the marinade, shaking off the excess marinade, and place it on the grill grate. Cook for 10 to 12 minutes for a butterflied leg or 2 minutes for lamb slices, brushing or spooning some of the reserved marinade on top. Flip the lamb over, brush or spoon the remaining reserved marinade on top, and cook for 10 to 12 minutes longer for a leg or 2 minutes longer for slices, until lightly charred.

Transfer the leg to a cutting board or the slices to a serving platter and let rest for 4 minutes. If you have cooked a whole leg, carve it against the grain into ¼-inch-thick slices and arrange on a serving platter. Serve the lamb hot.

KUNG FU IT Be sure to buy thick (can't-get-it-off-the-spoon) Greek yogurt for this recipe, as it helps the marinade cling to the meat. If you can't find Greek yogurt, strain regular yogurt as directed on page 24.

Korean Beef Satay

Flank steak is inexpensive compared to most steaks and is available at most grocery store meat counters. The Korean way to prepare relatively tough cuts like flank steak is to use a marinade that is both flavorful and a tenderizer. The enzymes in the kiwi and the Asian pear in the Korean BBQ Sauce both tenderize the meat and allow more of the spicy, sesame, and fennel flavors of the Magic Paste to penetrate. When this satay comes off the grill, it tastes like "beef kimchi"—it has that much flavor.

—

- ½ cup Magic Paste (page 44)
- 1 cup Korean BBQ Sauce (page 34)

1 cup sliced green onion, white and green parts

1 (3-inch) piece lemongrass, minced

3 pounds beef flank steak, sliced against the grain into pieces that are 6 inches long and 1 inch wide

PREP TIME 5 minutes
MARINATE TIME 20 minutes
COOK TIME 4 minutes
FEEDS 6 people

You will need 12 skewers, either wooden or metal, each 8 inches long. If you are using wooden skewers, soak them in water for at least 30 minutes or until you are ready to use them.

Combine the Magic Paste, BBQ sauce, green onions, and lemongrass in a large, shallow dish and mix well. Add the flank steak and turn the steak to coat evenly. Cover and marinate in the refrigerator for 20 minutes.

Heat the grill for direct heat cooking to medium (350°F to 375°F).

Remove the flank steak from the marinade, reserving the marinade. Thread 2 pieces of meat lengthwise onto each skewer, weaving the point of the skewer through the top, middle, and bottom of each piece, then pushing the pieces into an "S" shape, so they are touching. Pour the reserved marinade into a small saucepan, bring to a boil on the stove top or on the grill, and boil for a couple of minutes. Pour into a small heatproof bowl and set aside to use as a dipping sauce.

Place the skewers on the grill grate and cook, turning them once, for about 2 minutes on each side, until lightly charred.

Transfer the satay to a serving platter and let it rest for 3 minutes, then serve with the dipping sauce.

BBQ Meats

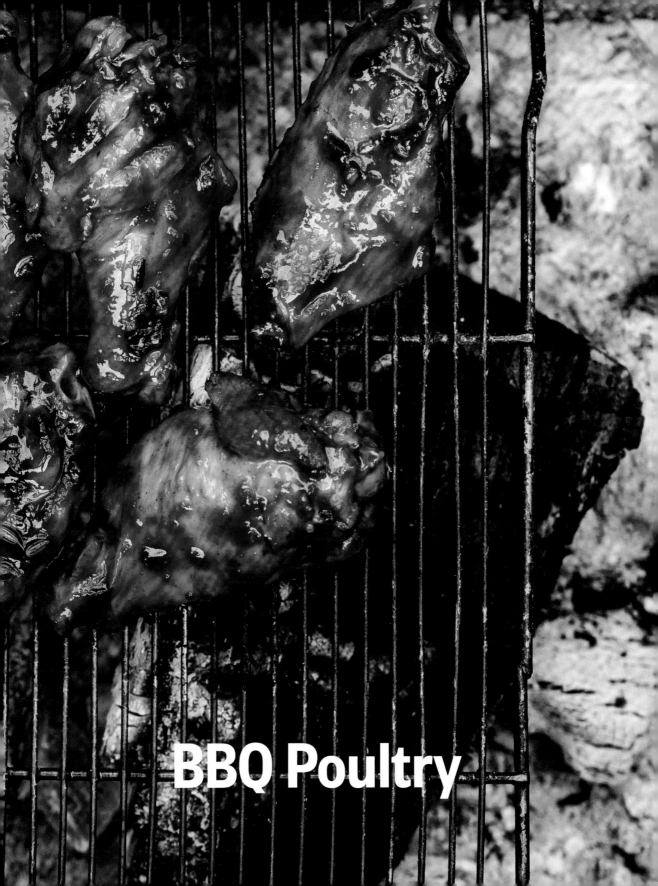

BBQ Poultry

While Korean barbecued beef and lamb tend to rely on robust, thick sauces, I like to use lighter, more acidic marinades and sauces for chicken and turkey. They have milder flavors, making them like blank slates that take on other flavors, so you don't want to pair them with anything heavy.

Chicken is very popular in South Korea. In cities like Seoul and Suwon, there are areas called "chicken alley" that are lined with restaurants specializing in fried or barbecue chicken. You'll also find stews of chicken and daikon or potatoes everywhere. Korean cooks get all they can out of the bird, using every piece of meat and cooking up flavorful broths from the bones. When I was growing up, my mom would buy bricks of Golden Curry brand curry paste and make our family chicken curry with potatoes and carrots, the same hearty, sunny-colored dish served in the curry houses found in most Japanese train stations. It was one of my favorite meals as a kid, and my nostalgia for that curried chicken stew is part of how I cook today, even if I prefer to grill my chicken.

We still eat a lot of chicken at home, and in this chapter you'll find our go-to recipes for everything from a football tailgate party to my mother-in-law's famous *lechon* Thanksgiving turkey.

BBQ Spiced Chicken Thighs with Yogurt Nuoc Cham Sauce

My wife, Yvonne, loves chicken, so this recipe is for her. She also likes her chicken cooked until it's a little burned—oh boy! She adores the charred flavors and all the crispy edges. I think it's because she's Puerto Rican and loves *chicharrones*. Because she likes it both crispy and juicy, I use chicken thighs, which are forgiving if you overcook them slightly by mistake. The sugar in the BBQ Spice Rub helps caramelize the edges of the chicken.

—

- ■ ¼ cup BBQ Spice Rub (page 52)
- ■ 1 cup Lemongrass Chili Sauce (page 36)
- ½ cup gochujang
- 4 pounds boneless, skin-on chicken thighs
- 2 cups plain Greek yogurt
- ■ 1 cup Nuoc Cham Sauce (page 42)
- 1 tablespoon Korean chili flakes
- 1 tablespoon kosher salt

PREP TIME 10 minutes
MARINATE TIME 45 minutes
COOK TIME 18 minutes
FEEDS 6 people

Combine the spice rub, chili sauce, and gochujang in a large bowl and mix well. Add the chicken thighs and turn to coat evenly. Cover and marinate in the refrigerator for 45 minutes.

Combine the yogurt, Nuoc Cham Sauce, chili flakes, and salt in a bowl and whisk together to make a dipping sauce. Cover and refrigerate until you are ready to use it.

Heat the grill for indirect heat cooking to medium (350°F to 375°F). (If using a charcoal grill, rake the coals to one side of the charcoal grate; if using a gas grill, turn off half of the burners.)

Place the chicken thighs, skin side down, on the grill grate directly over the fire. Cook, turning the thighs once, for 2 minutes on each side. Move the chicken away from the heat, close the lid, and cook, flipping the thighs over every 6 minutes so they cook evenly, for 18 minutes total, until cooked through. Don't let the meat char too much (unless you are cooking this for someone like Yvonne!).

Transfer the chicken to a serving platter and let rest for 5 minutes, then serve with the dipping sauce.

Lola's Thanksgiving Turkey

We have two Thanksgivings each year, a Korean one with braised short ribs and a Puerto Rican one with *lechon* turkey tenderloin served with *chimichurri*. Because we usually have only four people at my mother-in-law's house to devour this feast, we don't roast a whole bird. The tenderloin is marinated and cooks in no time, and we have leftovers for a couple of turkey sandwiches the next day. There's no need to wait for Thanksgiving or even to use turkey for this recipe. Pork tenderloin or even boneless chicken breasts are delicious prepared this way, too.

___

2 turkey breast tenderloins, about 1½ pounds each

■ 1¼ cups Ko-Rican Sauce (page 40)

■ ¼ cup Nuoc Cham Sauce (page 42)

1 tablespoon sambal oelek

¼ cup coarsely chopped fresh curly parsley

¼ cup coarsely chopped fresh cilantro

PREP TIME 20 minutes
MARINATE TIME 20 minutes to 1 hour
COOK TIME 25 minutes
FEEDS 6 people

Place the tenderloins in a large, shallow dish, pour 1 cup of the Ko-Rican Sauce over them, and turn the tenderloins to coat evenly. Cover and marinate in the refrigerator for at least 20 minutes or up to 1 hour.

Heat the grill for indirect heat cooking to medium (350°F to 375°F). (If using a charcoal grill, rake the coals to one side of the charcoal grate; if using a gas grill, turn off half of the burners.)

Place the tenderloins on the grill grate away from the heat, close the lid, and cook for 25 minutes, until the internal temperature reaches 165°F. If desired, just before the turkey has finished cooking, move it directly over the fire to brown, turning as needed. Transfer the turkey to a cutting board and let rest for 10 minutes.

While the turkey is cooking, make the Korean *chimichurri*. Combine the remaining ¼ cup Ko-Rican Sauce, Nuoc Cham Sauce, sambal oelek, parsley, and cilantro in a food processor and process for 1 minute, until smooth. Set the *chimichurri* aside at room temperature until the turkey is done.

Cut the tenderloins against the grain into ½-inch-thick slices and arrange on a serving platter. Accompany with the *chimichurri*.

KUNG FU IT You can make the base for the *chimichurri* (without the herbs) a week in advance. Stir in the herbs when you are ready to use it.

Lemongrass Chicken

I think we've lost the art of cooking chicken on the bone. The bones impart flavor to the meat and help the meat cook evenly. For this recipe, you're going to cook the chicken in the sauce in foil packets, so the chicken braises in the sweet sauce as it slowly cooks on the grill. The foil packet keeps the meat moist while cooking it evenly. Make sure you use heavy-duty foil in this recipe, and at least two layers of it.

■ 2 tablespoons Curry Salt (page 50)

■ 2 tablespoons Blackening Seasoning (page 48)

4 pounds bone-in, skin-on chicken breast, thighs, and drumsticks, in any combination

■ 2 cups Lemongrass Chili Sauce (page 36)

1 lemon, halved

PREP TIME 20 minutes
MARINATE TIME 1 hour
COOK TIME 45 minutes
FEEDS 6 people

Combine the Curry Salt and Blackening Seasoning in a small bowl and stir to mix. Season the chicken on both sides with the mixture, placing the pieces on a large sheet pan as they are coated. Cover and marinate in the refrigerator for 1 hour.

Heat the grill for indirect heat cooking to medium (350°F to 375°F). (If using a charcoal grill, rake the coals to one side of the charcoal grate; if using a gas grill, turn off half of the burners.)

Stack two good-size sheets of heavy-duty aluminum foil on a work surface. Place 3 pieces of the chicken in a single layer in the center of the foil. Spoon some of the chili sauce over the chicken, coating both sides, and then bring the sides of the foil together, wrapping the chicken tightly and sealing the edges and corners securely to make sure no liquid will escape. Repeat with the remaining chicken and chili sauce, using 3 pieces of chicken for each packet.

Place the foil packets on the grill grate away from the heat, close the lid, and cook for 45 minutes. Check the temperature of the cooked chicken by pushing a meat thermometer through the foil; don't try to unwrap the chicken first. Transfer the packets from the grill to a counter or work surface and let rest for 10 minutes.

Open the packets, working carefully because the steam is hot, and transfer the chicken to a serving platter. Spoon the sauce from the packets over the chicken, squeeze the lemon halves over the top, and serve.

Sesame Hoisin Chicken Wings

I'm a big sports fan, so great tailgating food is important to me (especially if your team is dogging it with bad plays). I like to use smaller wings and/or drumettes because they are more tender than the monster-size ones you get at a lot of bars. Keep an eye on the wings while they are cooking, as they can char quickly because of the sugar in the marinade. If they start to brown too much, move them to a cooler part of the grill to finish cooking.

—

- ½ cup Soy Balsamic Sauce (page 38)
- ¼ cup Magic Paste (page 44)

¼ cup hoisin sauce

½ cup thinly sliced green onions, white and green parts

3 pounds chicken wings and drumettes

Korean chili flakes (optional)

PREP TIME 15 minutes
MARINATE TIME 1 hour
COOK TIME 20 minutes
FEEDS 6 people

In a large bowl, combine the Soy Balsamic Sauce, Magic Paste, hoisin sauce, and green onions and mix well. Measure out ½ cup of the marinade and reserve for basting the wings on the grill. Place the chicken wings and drumettes in a large, shallow dish, pour the remaining marinade on top, and turn the wings and drumettes to coat evenly. Cover and marinate in the refrigerator for 1 hour.

Heat the grill for indirect heat cooking to medium (350°F to 375°F). (If using a charcoal grill, rake the coals to one side of the charcoal grate; if using a gas grill, turn off half of the burners.)

Place the wings and drumettes on the grill grate away from the heat, close the lid, and cook for 5 minutes. Flip the wings and drumettes over, baste them with some of the reserved marinade, close the lid, and cook for another 5 minutes. Flip the wings and drumettes over two more times, moving them directly over the fire, basting, and cooking for 5 minutes on each side. Sprinkle on some Korean chili flakes, if you like things a little spicier.

Transfer the wings and drumettes to a platter and serve.

Gochujang Sticky Chicken Drumsticks

When I was a kid and at the park grilling with my family, I always grabbed the chicken drumstick because I could hold it with one hand and a cup of Tang with the other and run around the park. I skip the Tang these days, but I always make more of these drumsticks than I need so there are leftovers. These are my go-to ultimate late night eat-standing-in-front-of-the-fridge food.

———

3 pounds chicken drumsticks

3 tablespoons Curry Salt (page 50)

1 cup Korean Pesto (page 46)

¼ cup Magic Paste (page 44)

¼ cup gochujang

PREP TIME 15 minutes
MARINATE TIME 1 hour
COOK TIME 25 minutes
FEEDS 6 people

Place the drumsticks in a large, shallow dish and season them evenly with the Curry Salt. Combine the pesto, Magic Paste, and gochujang in a small bowl and whisk until well mixed. Measure out ½ cup of the marinade and reserve for basting the drumsticks on the grill. Pour the remaining marinade over the drumsticks and turn to coat evenly. Cover and marinate in the refrigerator for 1 hour.

Heat the grill for direct heat cooking to medium-high (400°F to 450°F).

Place the drumsticks on the grill grate, close the lid, and cook for 3 minutes. Baste the drumsticks with some of the reserved marinade, turn them over, close the lid, and cook for another 3 minutes. Repeat flipping and basting the drumsticks three more times, closing the lid each time and grilling them for a total of 25 minutes.

Transfer the drumsticks to a serving platter, let them rest for 5 minutes, and serve.

Kaffir Lime Curry Chicken

My trip to Thailand is a memory that stays on my mind, in the best possible way. I still think about the food, from rustic stalls on roadsides and tiny cafés to meals in people's homes. The flavors also stay with me, especially lemongrass and kaffir lime leaves, and the mint, cilantro, Thai basil, and many other herbs that make Thai food so memorable. This recipe takes me back to Thailand every time I make it.

—

3 pounds boneless, skin-on chicken thighs

▧ 2 tablespoons Curry Salt (page 50)

■ 1 cup Korean Pesto (page 46)

5 kaffir lime leaves, coarsely chopped

■ 1 cup Lemongrass Chili Sauce (page 36)

Lettuce cups or lightly grilled pita breads, for serving

PREP TIME 10 minutes
MARINATE TIME 1¾ hours
COOK TIME 10 to 12 minutes
FEEDS 6 people

Place the chicken thighs in a large, shallow dish and season them evenly with the Curry Salt. Cover and marinate in the refrigerator for 1 hour.

Place the pesto and lime leaves in a food processor and process for 30 seconds, until smooth. Add the chili sauce and pulse to combine. Measure out ½ cup of the marinade and reserve for basting the chicken on the grill. Pour the remaining marinade over the chicken thighs and turn to coat evenly. Re-cover and marinate in the refrigerator for 45 minutes.

Heat the grill for direct heat cooking to medium (350°F to 375°F).

Place the chicken thighs, skin side down, on the grill grate, baste with some of the reserved marinade, close the lid, and cook for 4 to 6 minutes. Flip the chicken over, baste again, close the lid, and cook for another 4 to 6 minutes, until lightly charred.

Transfer the chicken to a serving platter and let rest for 5 minutes, then serve with the lettuce cups or grilled pita bread.

Curried Chicken Burgers

This is our version of a burger at Casa de Kim, which is what Yvonne and I call our house. I like eating these with lettuce cups, adding mint or basil and sometimes tomatoes. It's our way to enjoy a burger without feeling sluggish and heavy afterward.

—

2 pounds ground chicken thigh meat

■ ½ cup Korean Pesto (page 46)

■ 1 tablespoon Magic Paste (page 44)

¾ cup finely chopped white onion

1½ cups finely chopped napa cabbage

■ 1 tablespoon Curry Salt (page 50)

¼ cup panko (Japanese bread crumbs)

1 egg, lightly beaten

Lettuce cups, for serving

Assorted fresh herbs (such as mint and basil), for serving

PREP TIME 30 minutes
COOK TIME 10 to 12 minutes
FEEDS 6 people

Heat the grill for direct heat cooking to medium (350°F to 375°F).

Combine the chicken, pesto, Magic Paste, onion, cabbage, Curry Salt, panko, and egg in a large bowl and mix together gently but thoroughly. Divide the mixture into 6 equal portions and form each portion into a patty ½ inch thick. The patties will be really soft when you form them, but they will firm up once they are on the grill.

Place the patties on the grill, close the lid, and cook for 4 to 6 minutes. Flip the patties over, close the lid, and cook for another 4 to 6 minutes, until they are lightly charred and reach an internal temperature of 165°F.

Remove the burgers from the grill, let them rest for 5 minutes, and then serve with the lettuce cups and herbs.

Coconut-Peanut-Pesto Chicken Satay

This is one of the most popular orders at our restaurants; people can't get enough of the combination of coconut, peanut, and chicken. Although here it is served as satay, you can cook the chicken pieces whole and pair them with anything from ramen to tortilla chips to rice to salad.

———

2 pounds boneless, skinless chicken breasts, cut into 1-inch-thick slices

3 tablespoons olive oil

■ 1 tablespoon Blackening Seasoning (page 48)

1 tablespoon kosher salt

¼ cup coconut milk

■ ¼ cup Korean Pesto (page 46)

2 tablespoons smooth peanut butter

1 tablespoon sambal oelek

PREP TIME 20 minutes
COOK TIME 8 minutes
FEEDS 4 people

You will need 8 skewers, either wooden or metal, each 8 inches long. If you are using wooden skewers, soak them in water for at least 30 minutes or until you are ready to use them.

Thread 2 pieces of chicken lengthwise onto each skewer, weaving the point of the skewer through the top, middle, and bottom of each piece, then pushing the pieces into an "S" shape, so they are touching. Place them in a large, shallow dish. Drizzle the oil over the chicken and turn to coat evenly. Season the chicken with the Blackening Seasoning and salt, again coating evenly, then cover and refrigerate until the grill is ready.

Combine the coconut milk, pesto, peanut butter, and sambal oelek in a small bowl and whisk until well mixed to make a dressing. Set aside.

Heat the grill for direct heat cooking to medium-high (400°F to 450°F).

Place the chicken skewers on the grill grate, close the lid, and cook for 4 minutes. Flip the skewers over and cook for another 4 minutes, until they are lightly charred and reach an internal temperature of 165°F.

Transfer the satay to a serving platter, let rest for 4 minutes, and then serve with the peanut-pesto dressing on the side.

Korean Chicken Saltimbocca

Saltimbocca is not at all Korean, of course. It is one of those classic Italian dishes I remember eating at my friends' houses while growing up in one of the Italian neighborhoods in Chicago. Some cooks season saltimbocca with chili flakes, but instead I use Magic Paste, which gives it a nice kick.

—

6 (8-ounce) chicken cutlets

4 tablespoons Magic Paste (page 44)

1 tablespoon minced fresh sage (about 6 large leaves), plus 4 whole leaves

2 tablespoons olive oil

6 slices prosciutto

3 tablespoons unsalted butter

¼ cup dry white wine

¾ cup low-sodium chicken broth

PREP TIME 20 minutes
MARINATE TIME 20 minutes
COOK TIME 8 to 10 minutes
FEEDS 6 people

Soak 12 wooden toothpicks in water for 10 minutes or until you are ready to use them.

Place the chicken cutlets in a large, shallow dish, add 3 tablespoons of the Magic Paste, the minced sage, and the oil, and turn the chicken to coat evenly. Cover and marinate in the refrigerator for 20 minutes.

Heat the grill for direct heat cooking to medium-high (400°F to 450°F).

When the grill is ready, lay a prosciutto slice on top of each chicken cutlet and roll up the cutlet as if you were rolling up a yoga mat. Secure each roll with 2 toothpicks, one on each end.

Place the rolls on the grill grate, close the lid, and cook for 4 to 5 minutes. Turn the chicken over and cook for another 4 to 5 minutes, until the rolls are lightly charred and reach an internal temperature of 165°F. Transfer the chicken to a serving platter and let rest while you make the sauce.

Melt 1½ tablespoons of the butter in a small saucepan over medium heat. Add the whole sage leaves and the remaining 1 tablespoon Magic Paste and cook for 1 minute. Add the wine, bring to a boil, and boil until the wine reduces and the sauce is almost dry. Add the broth and simmer for 2 minutes. Whisk in the remaining 1½ tablespoons butter just until melted, then pour over the chicken and serve.

KUNG FU IT This recipe calls for chicken cutlets, which are thin pieces of boneless, skinless chicken breast. If you cannot find cutlets at the store, buy regular boneless, skinless chicken breasts and pound them between two pieces of waxed or parchment paper until about ¼ inch thick.

Lemongrass Chicken Egg Salad

I ate a lot of hard-boiled eggs as a kid while playing at the golf course with my brother and my dad. We were always starving by the ninth hole, and for some reason, there was always someone there selling hard-boiled eggs with salt and mustard packets. I never understood why they sold eggs as snacks for golfers, but they would tide us over until we were finished with the eighteenth hole and could go get a hot dog with all the fixings.

—

2 pounds boneless, skinless chicken breasts

1¼ cups Lemongrass Chili Sauce (page 36)

2 tablespoons sambal oelek

1 clove garlic, minced

Juice of 1 lime

¼ cup coarsely chopped fresh cilantro

4 celery stalks, thinly sliced

6 hard-boiled eggs, peeled and coarsely chopped

3 ripe avocados, halved, pitted, peeled, and coarsely chopped

6 sandwich buns, rice crackers, or toasted bread slices

PREP TIME 10 minutes
MARINATE TIME 1 to 12 hours
COOK TIME 8 minutes
FEEDS 6 people

Combine the chicken and 1 cup of the chili sauce in a large, shallow dish and turn the chicken to coat evenly. Cover and marinate in the refrigerator for at least 1 hour or up to overnight.

Heat the grill for direct heat grilling to medium-high (400°F to 450°F).

Place the chicken breasts on the grill grate, close the lid, and cook for 4 minutes. Flip the breasts over and cook for another 4 minutes, until they are lightly charred and reach an internal temperature of 165°F. Transfer the chicken to a cutting board, let rest for 5 minutes, and then chop into small pieces.

Combine the remaining ¼ cup chili sauce, sambal oelek, garlic, lime juice, cilantro, celery, eggs, avocado, and chopped chicken in a large bowl and stir gently until thoroughly mixed. Spoon the chicken egg salad into the buns and serve.

BBQ Fish and Shellfish

When I first came to America and had fish sticks in school, I didn't even realize they were fish because the taste was so mild.

That's not what we ate at home, of course. We'd go to Korean markets for beltfish, a long fish that looks like an eel, or for squid for my mom's spicy stir-fries. Sometimes my mom would cure pollock roe in salt for a couple of weeks, and we would eat it on rice with sesame oil and green onions. We also ate a lot of strong-flavored oily fish like mackerel, and we even ate barracuda (which is kind of weird when I think about it now). Once or twice a year, my mom would stuff raw crabs with rice and let them ferment for a week, which was a huge treat to me. (And yes, that seems weird now, too.)

Today, I love to cook fish and shellfish on the grill. Some of them, like shrimp and catfish, are light and mild, so I add rich, deep flavors with spice rubs, marinades, and sauces.

BBQ Fish and Shellfish

Seoul to Buffalo Shrimp

Shrimp are one of my favorite things to eat for dinner. They are quick and easy to cook and easy to find at our local supermarket. This is a Korean take on Buffalo shrimp, which means the sauce is sweet, spicy, and a little sticky. I prefer 16/20 count shrimp. The numbers, which are linked to size, refer to how many shrimp on average are in a pound; the higher the number, the smaller the shrimp. You want good-size shrimp for this recipe so they don't overcook and are easy to handle on the grill.

—

- 1½ cups Lemongrass Chili Sauce (page 36)

⅓ cup unsalted butter, melted

2 tablespoons white sesame seeds, toasted

2 tablespoons sambal oelek

3 pounds extra-large peeled and deveined shrimp (16/20 count)

- ¼ cup Blackening Seasoning (page 48)

PREP TIME 10 minutes
COOK TIME 4 minutes
FEEDS 6 people

Heat the grill for direct heat cooking to medium (350°F to 375°F).

Combine the chili sauce, butter, sesame seeds, and sambal oelek in a large bowl and whisk until well mixed. Set aside.

When the grill is ready, season the shrimp with the Blackening Seasoning, coating them evenly. Place the shrimp on the grill grate, close the lid, and cook for 2 minutes. Flip the shrimp over, close the lid, and cook them for another 2 minutes, until they turn an opaque pink color.

Remove the shrimp from the grill, add to the sauce, toss well, and serve.

Korean BBQ Salmon

You can cook the salmon in a grill pan or directly on the grill grate for this recipe, but you'll need to cook the vegetables in a grill pan. Be sure to preheat the pan so the marinade caramelizes while the vegetables cook. That intense heat brings out the flavors and makes them pop. As I mentioned in the Tools section (see page 15), I prefer a ceramic grill pan, as it heats well and is easy to clean afterward.

—

2 cups sliced white mushrooms

½ cup sliced green onions, white and green parts

1 small yellow onion, sliced

■ 3 cups Korean BBQ Sauce (page 34), or more if needed

3 pounds skinless salmon fillet, cut into 3-ounce pieces

PREP TIME 10 minutes
MARINATE TIME 1 hour
COOK TIME 13 minutes
FEEDS 6 people

Combine the mushrooms, green onions, yellow onion, and BBQ sauce in a large, shallow dish and mix well. Add the salmon and turn to coat evenly. Cover and marinate in the refrigerator for 1 hour.

Place a grill pan on the grill grate, then heat the grill for direct heat cooking to medium-high (400°F to 450°F).

Spoon the marinated vegetables onto the grill pan and cook for 8 minutes, stirring the vegetables occasionally and adding more sauce to the grill pan if the vegetables dry out. While the vegetables are cooking, place the salmon on the grill grate, close the lid, and cook for 2 minutes. Flip the salmon over, close the lid, and cook for 3 minutes more, until the salmon is lightly charred.

Remove the salmon from the grill and arrange on a platter with the vegetables and serve.

Spicy Grilled Crabs

We used to eat blue crabs when I was a kid, but we didn't grill them. My mom would ferment them, then stuff them with rice and we'd eat them. She didn't prepare these crabs very often, so it was considered a special occasion when she did. As a kid, I loved them, but looking back, I don't know that I would eat that again. But this version of grilled crabs still takes me back to my mom's kitchen, when I would peek into the dish to see if the crabs were ready. I like to stuff the shells with cooked rice after they come off the grill; the rice picks up some of the crab flavor while also soaking up the butter and Korean pesto. You can make this recipe with crab legs if you prefer, which is a lot less work.

---

12 live whole blue crabs, measuring about 4 to 5 inches across (see note), or 4 pounds crab legs

- ¾ cup Magic Paste (page 44)

¾ cup olive oil

3 cups cooked rice (optional)

4 tablespoons unsalted butter, melted

- ¼ cup Korean Pesto (page 46)

4 lemons, cut into wedges

PREP TIME 45 minutes
MARINATE TIME 1 hour
COOK TIME 13 minutes
FEEDS 6 people

First, if you are using whole crabs, clean them: Immerse the crabs in ice water for 6 minutes (watch out for the claws!). Then, one at a time, hold each crab by the bottom, shell side down, and using a towel to protect your fingers, twist off the two large claws, and place them in a bowl. Lift up the apron (the triangular flap), then twist it to pull it off. Flip the crab over and pry off the top shell. Remove the gills and guts. You might see some bright orange stuff, which is the roe. If you find roe, scoop it out, and set it aside in the refrigerator to eat with the crab or later over rice—it's delicious. Then rinse the crab under cold running water. If you are using large crabs, cut each crab in half vertically. If you are using crab legs, using a pair of kitchen shears, cut down one side of each leg to expose the meat. Place the crabs in a baking dish and cover them with wet paper towels.

Combine the Magic Paste and oil in a small bowl and mix well. Brush the mixture evenly over the crabs. Cover and marinate in the refrigerator for 1 hour.

Heat the grill for direct heat cooking to medium (350°F to 375°F).

CONTINUED

Spicy Grilled Crabs

CONTINUED

Place the crabs on the grill grate and cook, turning once, for 5 minutes on each side. If you are using crab legs, cook them for only 2 minutes on each side. Move the crabs or crab legs to a cooler area of the grill (to the edge of the rack if using a charcoal grill or turn off one burner if using a gas grill) and let them cook for 3 minutes longer, until the shells brown slightly.

Transfer the crabs or crab legs to a large serving platter and stuff the shells with the rice. In a small bowl, whisk together the butter and pesto to make a dipping sauce. Squeeze the lemons over the crabs, then serve the crabs with the dipping sauce and reserved roe if you like.

NOTE You can buy live blue crabs at Asian markets, just don't let the crabs escape and crawl around your car! Make sure you don't handle the crabs too much (you don't want them to start fighting you), and get them into a refrigerator as quickly as possible.

Korean BBQ

Smoky Catfish with Soy-Chipotle Sauce

Catfish is hugely underrated in America. I like it for its firm texture and because it takes on seasonings and marinades well, similar to the way meat does. In this recipe, the catfish gets nice and smoky on the grill with help from the Blackening Seasoning and chipotle chilies, plus it's a little sweet and spicy from the Korean BBQ Sauce. I like to serve this catfish with sautéed greens and dirty rice.

—

6 (6-ounce) catfish fillets

■ 1 cup Blackening Seasoning (page 48)

■ 1½ cups Korean BBQ Sauce (page 34)

3 chipotle chilies in adobo sauce, plus 1 tablespoon adobo sauce

PREP TIME 10 minutes
MARINATE TIME 20 minutes
COOK TIME 6 to 8 minutes
FEEDS 6 people

Place the catfish in a large, shallow dish and season with the Blackening Seasoning, coating evenly. Place the BBQ sauce and the chipotle chilies and adobo sauce in a food processor and blend for about 30 seconds, until smooth. Pour the marinade over the catfish and turn to coat evenly. Cover and marinate in the refrigerator for 20 minutes.

Meanwhile, heat the grill for direct heat cooking to medium (350°F to 375°F).

Place the catfish on the grill grate, close the lid, and cook for 3 to 4 minutes. Using a large spatula, carefully flip the catfish over, close the lid again, and cook for 3 to 4 minutes more, until lightly charred.

Remove the catfish from the grill and serve immediately.

NOTE I always use fresh catfish—never frozen. Fresh catfish has more flavor and a firmer texture, which makes it easier to cook. You can find fresh catfish in many grocery stores and Asian markets.

Trout with Citrus Nuoc Cham Butter

I like to grill trout with seasoned butter in foil packets. That way, you get all the juice and flavors but no mess. The lettuce and tomatoes pick up the flavors of the seasoned butter and taste incredible. You can assemble the foil packages up to eight hours in advance and store them in the refrigerator until you're ready to grill.

---

1 cup unsalted butter, at room temperature

Grated or minced zest of 1 lemon

3 tablespoons fresh lemon juice

■ ¼ cup Nuoc Cham Sauce (page 42)

■ 2 teaspoons Curry Salt (page 50)

3 heads romaine lettuce, cored and coarsely chopped

6 (8-ounce) trout fillets

1 pint cherry tomatoes, halved

PREP TIME 30 minutes
CHILL TIME 2 hours
COOK TIME 15 minutes
FEEDS 6 people

Place the butter, lemon zest and juice, Nuoc Cham Sauce, and 1 teaspoon of the Curry Salt in a food processor and process for about 1 minute, until thoroughly blended. Scrape the butter out of the food processor onto a large sheet of plastic wrap, forming it into a rough log. Using the plastic wrap, mold the butter into a smooth, uniform log about 6 inches long, then wrap the log tightly in the plastic wrap and twist the ends to secure. Place the butter in the refrigerator for 2 hours to firm up (if you're short on time, slip it into the freezer for 30 minutes).

Heat the grill for direct heat cooking to medium (350°F to 375°F).

Lay out two sheets of aluminum foil, each about 18 inches long, on a work surface. Divide the chilled butter into 12 equal pieces. Divide the lettuce evenly between the foil sheets. Place 3 trout fillets on top of each bed of lettuce, season them with the remaining 1 teaspoon Curry Salt, and top each fillet with the tomatoes and 2 pieces of the seasoned butter. Bring up the sides of the foil and wrap loosely around the fish, folding the edges and crimping the seams to seal the packets closed.

When the grill is ready, place the foil packages on the grill grate, close the lid, and cook for 12 to 15 minutes, until a thin skewer inserted into one of the fillets comes out warm. Remove the packets from the grill and let rest for 5 minutes before opening.

Open the packets and transfer the trout and vegetables to plates. Serve with the remaining pieces of seasoned butter.

BBQ Fish and Shellfish

Blackened Salmon Po' Boys

This is my homage to the seafood po' boys I eat every time I go to New Orleans. These iconic sandwiches are served on baguettes, but what many people don't know is that the big Vietnamese population in New Orleans uses rice flour to make the baguettes for their po' boys and their *bahn mi*, their traditional sandwiches. I take that adaptation a step further and use crispy rice cakes as the base for an open-faced sandwich. Feel free to use a baguette or even a hamburger bun in place of the rice cakes.

—

2½ pounds skinless salmon fillet, cut into 12 equal pieces

■ ½ cup Blackening Seasoning (page 48)

¼ cup mayonnaise

1 tablespoon hoisin sauce

■ 2 tablespoons Lemongrass Chili Sauce (page 36)

■ 1 cup Nuoc Cham Sauce (page 42)

1 cup plain Greek yogurt

¼ cup toasted sesame oil

2 tablespoons sambal oelek

1 tablespoon Korean chili flakes

1 cup shredded red cabbage

½ cup shredded carrots

1 seedless cucumber, thinly sliced

¼ cup coarsely chopped fresh cilantro

6 crispy rice cakes

PREP TIME 20 minutes
COOK TIME 5 minutes
FEEDS 6 people

Place a grill pan on the grill grate, then heat the grill for direct heat cooking to medium-high (400°F to 450°F).

While the grill is heating, season the salmon pieces with the Blackening Seasoning and set aside.

Whisk together the mayonnaise, hoisin sauce, and chili sauce in a small bowl, cover, and refrigerate until ready to use. Whisk together the Nuoc Cham Sauce, yogurt, sesame oil, sambal oelek, and chili flakes in a separate bowl to make a dressing. Place the cabbage, carrots, cucumbers, and cilantro in a large bowl, pour on the dressing, and toss until well mixed.

Place the salmon on the grill pan, close the lid, and cook for 3 minutes. Flip the salmon over, close the lid again, and cook for another 2 minutes, until lightly charred.

Place the rice cakes on a platter, and top each with a spoonful of the Asian slaw. Remove the salmon from the grill and place 2 pieces on top of each slaw-topped rice cake. Spoon a dollop of the mayo mixture on the salmon, and serve.

KUNG FU IT When you need very thinly sliced vegetables, like the cucumbers in this recipe, and you don't have a mandoline, you can use a vegetable peeler instead of a knife to get superthin slices. Just run the peeler down the length of the cucumber to get long, thin slices, and then cut them into smaller pieces.

Spicy Lemongrass Squid

My family ate a lot of squid when I was young, which, now that I think about it, was unusual for a kid in Chicago. Squid was a staple for us: we ate it steamed, grilled, and fried, but most often, we ate *ojingeo bokkeum*, which is spicy stir-fried squid. This recipe adds the Thai flavors of lemongrass and chili and is an easy way to start grilling squid. When buying squid, look for ones with shiny and plump (not flat) bodies and that smell like the ocean, two signs they are fresh. Most squid are sold cleaned of the head and ink sac and everything else, but if not, your fishmonger can clean them for you.

———

2 pounds cleaned squid

6 green onions, trimmed

1 yellow onion, quartered

½ cup Lemongrass Chili Sauce (page 36)

1 tablespoon soy sauce

3 tablespoons Korean chili flakes

PREP TIME 15 minutes
MARINATE TIME 40 minutes
COOK TIME 3 minutes
FEEDS 6 people

Place the squid, green onions, yellow onion, chili sauce, soy sauce, and chili flakes in a large, shallow dish and toss to combine. Cover and marinate in the refrigerator for 40 minutes.

Heat the grill for direct heat cooking to medium-high (400°F to 450°F).

Place the squid, green onions, and yellow onion on the grill grate and cook for 2 minutes, until the squid is firm and lightly charred. Transfer the squid and green onions to a cutting board to rest while the yellow onion wedges cook for 1 minute longer, until charred and softened. Remove them from the grill.

Cut the squid and green onions into 2-inch pieces, arrange on a serving platter with the yellow onion, and serve.

KUNG FU IT I like to combine the squid and onions hot off the grill with lettuce, sliced tomatoes, and a squeeze of lemon juice and then toss everything together. The marinade on the hot squid and onions combines with the lemon juice and the juice from the tomatoes to make a light dressing for the salad. It's like the squid salad I always order at Greek restaurants but with a little Korean kick.

BBQ Fish and Shellfish

Gun Bae Soju Scallops

One of the best parts of my last visit to South Korea was when Yvonne and I walked through the night market to check out all of the amazing street food. I still remember one vendor who was grilling scallops and glazing them with soy and honey. Eating these scallops always takes me right back to that night in Seoul. I use *soju*, a Korean liquor made from rice or other grains, in this recipe but if you can't find it, use rice vinegar, sake, or vodka. I like these scallops served over lettuce or with rice.

———

- ½ cup Soy Balsamic Sauce (page 38)
- 2 tablespoons soju
- 2 tablespoons olive oil
- 1 tablespoon Dijon mustard
- 1 tablespoon honey
- 1 teaspoon ground black pepper
- 24 large sea scallops

PREP TIME 5 minutes
MARINATE TIME 20 minutes
COOK TIME 4 minutes
FEEDS 6 people

Combine the Soy Balsamic Sauce, soju, oil, mustard, honey, and black pepper in a large bowl and whisk together until well mixed. Reserve ¼ cup of the marinade. Add the scallops to the remaining marinade and turn to coat evenly. Cover and marinate in the refrigerator for 20 minutes.

Heat the grill for direct heat cooking to medium-high (400°F to 450°F). Place the scallops over the hottest part of the grill and cook for 2 minutes. Brush them with the reserved marinade, flip them over, and cook them for another 2 minutes, until lightly charred and somewhat firm to the touch. Check them occasionally to make sure they don't overcook.

Transfer the scallops to a serving platter and serve.

NOTE When buying scallops, look for either diver or dry-packed scallops. Diver scallops, which are harvested by hand from the ocean floor, are my preferred choice. If you cannot find them, dry-packed scallops are the next best thing. Just don't buy wet, or soaked, scallops, which have been held in a chemical solution that adds water weight and turns them a bright white. They are also a little tougher and lack the sweet, briny taste of the ocean.

Gochujang Salmon

When I was in culinary school, I cooked at Le Titi de Paris, a formal French restaurant where I was in charge of making a classic Normandy-style sauce with cider, shallots, thyme, white wine vinegar, cream, and butter for salmon. It was the first time I tasted hard apple cider, and I really liked it, so I always snuck a sip or two while I was in the wine cellar getting the cider to make the sauce. That was twenty-five years ago, but I still think about those days whenever I make this salmon with apple juice or cider, except now I use *gochujang* instead of cream and butter, for a lighter, spicier dish. I like to eat this salmon with spicy watercress and sweet orange slices for contrast.

——

½ cup gochujang

¼ cup apple juice or hard cider

■ ¼ cup Korean BBQ Sauce (page 34)

¼ cup thinly sliced green onions, white and green parts

2 teaspoons ground black pepper

2 pounds skinless salmon fillet, cut into 5-ounce pieces

PREP TIME 10 minutes
MARINATE TIME 20 minutes
COOK TIME 6 minutes
FEEDS 6 people

Combine the gochujang, apple juice, BBQ sauce, green onions, and pepper in a small bowl and whisk together until well mixed. Reserve ¼ cup of the marinade. Place the salmon in a large, shallow dish, pour in the remaining marinade, and turn the salmon to coat evenly. Cover and marinate in the refrigerator for 20 minutes.

Heat the grill for indirect heat cooking to medium-high (400°F to 450°F). (If using a charcoal grill, rake the coals to one side of the charcoal grate; if using a gas grill, turn off half of the burners.)

Place the salmon directly over the fire, close the lid, and cook for 2 minutes. Using a large spatula, carefully flip the salmon over, close the lid again, and cook for another 2 minutes. Move the salmon away from the heat, close the lid, and cook for 2 more minutes, until lightly charred.

Transfer the salmon to a serving platter, spoon a small amount of the reserved marinade on top, and serve.

BBQ Fish and Shellfish

BBQ Vegetables and Tofu

As I get older, the recipes that inspire me most are the classic ones, and the memories that inspire me are of my family at home. My mom was a gardener, so vegetables were always a big part of our life. She grew Kirby cucumbers along the fence at our house on the northwest side of Chicago. When the cucumber flowers blossomed, we knew what was about to come. I remember that my brother, Mike, and I would fight over who got to pick the cucumbers first. Those were good times!

Mom couldn't grow her own napa cabbage, which was the only kind we knew, so every October she would buy a huge case of it and would invite her two sisters to come over to make kimchi in our kitchen. That was a family ritual for them and a connection back to Korea, where families were doing the same thing and making enough kimchi to tide them over until the next year. I didn't make kimchi, but I hung out nearby so I could taste the first batch.

I don't garden like my mom used to, but I still have a passion for vegetables. Grilling eggplant, cauliflower, and brussels sprouts totally changed how I feel about them, and I hope you'll feel as I do after trying some of these recipes.

Blackened BBQ Tofu

I think tofu is a missed opportunity for most people. People think it's a flavorless white brick, but it's so much more than that. I marinate it, blacken it, grill it, braise it, and fry it, just like any meat or fish, and it takes on an incredible amount of flavor when prepared correctly. When buying tofu, make sure the liquid in the package is clear, not cloudy, so you know it's fresh.

—

2 pounds firm or extra-firm tofu, drained and cut crosswise into 6 equal slices

■ 1 cup Korean BBQ Sauce (page 34)

½ cup sambal oelek

■ 2 tablespoons Blackening Seasoning (page 48)

PREP TIME 10 minutes
MARINATE TIME 20 minutes
COOK TIME 4 minutes
FEEDS 6 people

Arrange the tofu slices in a large, shallow dish. Combine the BBQ sauce and sambal oelek in a small bowl and whisk together until well mixed. Pour the sauce over the tofu, carefully turning the tofu to coat evenly. Marinate at room temperature for 20 minutes.

Heat the grill for direct heat cooking to medium (350°F to 375°F).

Remove the tofu from the marinade, reserving the marinade. Season the tofu on all sides with the Blackening Seasoning. Place the tofu on the grill grate, close the lid, and cook for 2 minutes. Using a large spatula, flip the tofu over, brush it with some of the reserved marinade, close the lid, and cook for another 2 minutes, until lightly charred.

Transfer the tofu to a serving platter and serve, with the reserved marinade on the side.

Tofu Joe Sandwiches

I was a big fan of Sloppy Joes as a kid, and learned to cook them when I was pretty young, since all you had to do was cook ground beef and open a can of sauce. Even now, I just love the name; it just makes me laugh. When I'm cooking, I like to take what people know and turn it upside down, like with this Korean tofu version of that nostalgic meal.

—

1 pound extra-firm tofu, drained

2 tablespoons extra-virgin olive oil

1 small yellow onion, diced

1 cup sliced white mushrooms

■ 3 tablespoons Magic Paste (page 44)

1 teaspoon chili powder

1 (15-ounce) can tomato sauce

½ cup coconut milk

½ cup drained canned chickpeas

■ ¼ cup Korean Pesto (page 46)

6 hamburger buns

PREP TIME 20 minutes
COOK TIME 23 to 28 minutes
FEEDS 6 people

Cut the block of tofu in half, cut each half lengthwise into 8 slices, and then chop the slices into small pieces. Set aside.

Place a grill pan on the grill grate, then heat the grill for indirect heat cooking to medium-high (400°F to 450°F). (If using a charcoal grill, rake the coals to one side of the charcoal grate; if using a gas grill, turn off half the burners.)

Heat the oil in the grill pan placed over the hottest part of the grill, then add the onion and mushrooms and cook, stirring occasionally, for about 5 minutes or until lightly charred. Add the Magic Paste and chili powder, stir well, and cook for 3 minutes. Add the tomato sauce, coconut milk, chickpeas, diced tofu, and pesto, stir well, move the pan away from the direct heat, close the lid, and cook at a slow simmer for 15 to 20 minutes, stirring every few minutes, until the liquid has thickened to the consistency of gravy.

Scoop the tofu Joe onto the bottoms of the buns, dividing it evenly, and then close with the tops and serve immediately.

Sizzling Soy Balsamic Portabello Mushrooms

Mushrooms cooked this way are meaty, juicy, and super tasty. You can eat them as a side, or you can use them to make all kinds of other dishes: chop and serve them on crostini or a pizza crust for an appetizer, put them on a bun for a vegetable burger, or slice them and serve them over noodles, rice, or salad. If you like, before grilling, use a spoon to scrape the gills from the portabellos, though it's not necessary.

—

10 medium-size portabello mushrooms, stemmed

½ cup vegetable oil

1 cup Soy Balsamic Sauce (page 38)

1 cup Korean BBQ Sauce (page 34)

PREP TIME 5 minutes
MARINATE TIME 20 minutes
COOK TIME 8 minutes
FEEDS 5 people

Place the mushrooms in a large, shallow dish. Combine the oil, Soy Balsamic Sauce, and BBQ sauce in a bowl and whisk together until well mixed. Pour the marinade over the mushrooms and turn the mushrooms to coat evenly. Marinate at room temperature for 20 minutes.

Heat the grill for direct heat cooking to medium (350°F to 375°F).

Remove the mushrooms from the marinade, reserving the marinade, and place them on the grill grate. Close the lid and cook for 2 minutes. Flip the mushrooms over, baste with some of the marinade, and cook for another 2 minutes. Repeat the flipping and basting two more times, closing the lid each time, until lightly charred.

Transfer the mushrooms to a serving platter and serve.

Cauliflower Steaks with Korean Pesto

When I first tasted fresh cauliflower, it blew my mind. If, like me, you grew up eating mushy, flavorless frozen cauliflower, this recipe will be a revelation. When sliced and grilled, cauliflower develops a deep, nutty flavor and nice grill marks, making it a satisfying vegetable steak.

---

2 large heads cauliflower

½ cup olive oil

■ 1 tablespoon Curry Salt (page 50)

■ 1 cup Korean Pesto (page 46)

PREP TIME 10 minutes
COOK TIME 8 minutes
FEEDS 6 people

Heat the grill for direct heat cooking to medium-high (400°F to 450°F).

Cut each cauliflower vertically into about 5 thick slices; the thickness will depend on how big the heads are. Brush the cauliflower steaks on both sides with the oil and then season on both sides with the Curry Salt.

Place the cauliflower slices on the grill grate, close the lid, and cook for 4 minutes. Flip the slices over, close the lid, and cook for another 4 minutes, until lightly charred.

Transfer the cauliflower to a serving platter, spoon the pesto on top, and serve.

Grilled Romaine with Feta and Nuoc Cham

If you've never eaten grilled lettuce, you're in for a nice surprise. When you grill a relatively hearty lettuce like romaine, the edges become crispy from the grill, not to mention tender and smoky. Grilling lettuce brings a whole new dimension to a vegetable you think you know well and turns a simple salad into something memorable. This recipe was inspired by a dish of grilled escarole with burned garlic, lemon juice, and good olive oil that I had at an Italian restaurant in Philadelphia. I couldn't get enough of it, and hope you feel the same about this grilled salad.

---

3 hearts romaine lettuce, halved lengthwise

2 tablespoons olive oil

¼ cup Nuoc Cham Sauce (page 42), at room temperature

½ cup crumbled feta cheese

¼ cup chopped fresh cilantro

PREP TIME 10 minutes
COOK TIME 3 minutes
FEEDS 6 people

Heat the grill for direct heat cooking to medium-high (400°F to 450°F).

Brush the lettuce with the oil. Place the romaine halves, cut side down, on the grill grate and cook for 1½ minutes. Flip the romaine over and grill for another 1½ minutes, until lightly charred.

Transfer the lettuce, cut side up, to a serving platter. Pour the Nuoc Cham Sauce over the romaine, top with the feta and cilantro, and serve.

Gochujang Asparagus

When I was a kid, we always—and I mean always—had Kirby cucumbers from my mother's garden on the dinner table. We ate them with *gochujang*, so when my mom first tried cooking asparagus, she served it in a similar style, with *gochujang* and vinegar, a mix of sweet and sour flavors. I wait all year for the first asparagus of the season so I can cook this dish. In the Midwest, that's anywhere from late April to early June, depending on the weather. I prefer the pencil-thin asparagus spears, but if you use those, you have to make sure you do not overcook them.

—

¼ cup gochujang

¼ cup distilled white vinegar

2 teaspoons sugar

2 tablespoons toasted sesame oil

1 clove garlic, minced

1 teaspoon black sesame seeds (use toasted white sesame seeds if you can't find black ones)

2 bunches asparagus, preferably pencil-thin, tough ends trimmed

1 tablespoon vegetable oil

■ 2 tablespoons Blackening Seasoning (page 48)

PREP TIME 15 minutes
COOK TIME 2 to 3 minutes
FEEDS 6 people

Heat the grill for direct heat cooking to medium (350°F to 375°F).

Combine the gochujang, vinegar, sugar, sesame oil, garlic, and sesame seeds in a bowl and whisk until well mixed. Set aside.

In a large, shallow dish, toss the asparagus with the vegetable oil, coating evenly, and then season evenly with the Blackening Seasoning. Place the asparagus on the grill grate and cook for 1 minute. Flip the asparagus over and cook for another minute if using thin spears or 2 minutes if using thick spears, until lightly charred.

Transfer the asparagus to a serving platter, toss with the gochujang sauce mixture, and serve.

KUNG FU IT Flipping asparagus on the grill takes a little practice. I think it's easier to do with tongs instead of a spatula. First, always make sure the spears are perpendicular to the grate bars, otherwise they'll just fall into the fire. Use the tongs to grab several spears at once and then turn them so the tips face the opposite direction. That's how you'll know which asparagus you've flipped and which asparagus you haven't. Don't try to grab too many spears at once, or you'll risk losing them through the grate.

Brussels Sprouts with Korean Pesto Butter

I hated brussels sprouts until we opened our second restaurant, Belly Shack, in 2009. We were testing different options for the menu, and I realized that I just hadn't had them cooked the right way. Boiled, they didn't have much flavor, but once I tried them sautéed, fried, roasted, or grilled, they became something entirely different. I love the texture brussels sprouts develop when grilled or roasted, with crunchy leaves on the outside and deep toasted flavors inside. These days, you can find roasted or fried brussels sprouts on lots of menus, most of the time cooked with bacon. But bacon can sometimes overwhelm the flavors of the sprouts, so I skip it here. Instead, you get all the tang and spice of the Korean Pesto, which is a nice partner for the sprouts.

½ cup unsalted butter, at room temperature

■ 2 tablespoons Korean Pesto (page 46)

2 pounds brussels sprouts, stems trimmed, then halved lengthwise

¼ cup olive oil

■ 1 tablespoon Curry Salt (page 50)

■ ¼ cup Nuoc Cham Sauce (page 42)

PREP TIME 20 minutes
CHILL TIME 2 hours
COOK TIME 12 minutes
FEEDS 6 people

Place the butter and pesto in a food processor and process for about 1 minute, until thoroughly mixed. Scrape the butter out of the food processor onto a large sheet of plastic wrap, forming it into a rough log. Using the plastic wrap, mold the butter into a smooth, uniform log about 6 inches long, then wrap the log tightly in the plastic wrap and twist the ends to secure. (See photos, next page.) Place the butter in the refrigerator for 2 hours to firm up (if you're short on time, slip it into the freezer for 30 minutes).

Place a grill pan on the grill grate, then heat the grill for direct heat cooking to medium-high (400°F to 450°F).

In a large bowl, toss the brussels sprouts with the oil, coating them evenly, then season then evenly with the Curry Salt. Remove the pesto butter from the refrigerator and cut it into 6 pieces.

Place the sprouts in a grilling basket, close the lid, and cook for 5 minutes, until browned. Flip the basket with the sprouts over, close the lid, and cook for 7 more minutes, until browned on the second side.

CONTINUED

Brussels Sprouts with Korean Pesto Butter

CONTINUED

Transfer the sprouts to a large bowl and add the Nuoc Cham Sauce and the pesto butter. Toss everything together until the butter melts, then serve.

NOTE Look for small brussels sprouts, as they are a little sweeter than large ones. It's okay if they have a few yellowed leaves, which you can remove. But stay away from sprouts that have a lot of yellowed leaves. That's the vegetable telling you it's getting old.

Grilled Chinese Eggplant

This is another recipe I have to credit to my mother, as she's the person who taught me that eggplant can steal the show in a recipe. When I was kid, I hated eggplant—the way it looked, the strange color. I once took a bite of raw eggplant and it tasted like unripe banana—gross! But then I learned how to cook it, and it became one of the staple vegetables in my cooking at our restaurants and at home. This recipe calls for long, slender Chinese or Japanese eggplants, which are most easily found at Asian markets and are less bitter and have thinner skin than the more common globe eggplant. Pick out firm ones with bright color and no blemishes.

---

3 Chinese eggplants, halved lengthwise

½ cup olive oil

1 tablespoon Curry Salt (page 50)

1 cups Nuoc Cham Sauce (page 42)

¼ cup toasted sesame oil

½ cup chopped fresh cilantro

1 small red onion, thinly sliced

1 lemon, halved

PREP TIME 10 minutes
COOK TIME 10 minutes
FEEDS 6 people

Heat the grill for direct heat cooking to medium (350°F to 375°).

Brush the eggplant halves with the olive oil, coating them evenly, and season evenly with the Curry Salt. Place the eggplants on the grill grate, close the lid, and cook for 5 minutes. Flip the eggplants over, close the lid, and cook for 5 more minutes, until lightly charred and tender.

Transfer the eggplants to a large, shallow dish. (You can leave them whole or you can slice them if you prefer.) Add the Nuoc Cham Sauce, sesame oil, cilantro, and onion and stir to mix everything together. Squeeze the lemon on top and serve.

Korean Elotes

The Mexican street dish called *elotes* was the inspiration for this recipe. Grill the corn first, then give it a dip in the seasoned butter to add layers of sweet, salty, and spicy flavors all at once. I like to use extra-hot prepared horseradish in this recipe because it has plenty of pungent, sharp, in-your-face flavor that mellows a bit in the butter but still delivers heat. Cut the corn kernels off the cob if you prefer this as a side dish (or if you don't want corn kernels stuck in your teeth after eating it).

—

½ cup unsalted butter, at room temperature

■ 2 tablespoons Magic Paste (page 44)

1 tablespoon extra-hot prepared horseradish

1 teaspoon kosher salt

6 ears corn, husked

¼ cup vegetable oil

■ 1 tablespoon Curry Salt (page 50)

PREP TIME 10 minutes
CHILL TIME 2 hours
COOK TIME 8 minutes
FEEDS 6 people

Place the butter, Magic Paste, horseradish, and kosher salt in a food processor and blend for about 30 seconds, until thoroughly mixed. Scrape the butter out of the food processor onto a large sheet of plastic wrap, forming it into a rough log. Using the plastic wrap, mold the butter into a smooth, uniform log about 6 inches long, then wrap the log tightly in the plastic wrap and twist the ends to secure. Place the butter in the refrigerator for 2 hours to firm up (if you're short on time, slip it into the freezer for 30 minutes).

Heat the grill for direct heat cooking to medium-high (400°F to 450°F). Remove the butter log from the refrigerator and cut it into 6 pieces.

Rub the corn with the oil and season it evenly with the Curry Salt. Place the corn on the grill grate, close the lid, and cook, turning it every 2 minutes, for a total of 8 minutes, until each side is lightly charred and tender.

Transfer the ears to a large, shallow dish, add the Magic Paste butter, and toss together until the butter melts. Let the corn swim in the butter a bit before serving it. You'll need plenty of napkins for this one!

Sides

What's a barbecue without sides? As much as I love barbecued meats, seafood, and vegetables, I always look forward to the side dishes, too. For me, one or two types of kimchi are a must; they add a lot of spice and punchy flavors to cut the fattiness of all of the meat that's usually served. That's the Korean influence. But I also like to Kung Fu some classic American barbecue sides, like baked beans, grits, and potato salad, giving them lighter, fresher flavors. And because the pickled red onions that you get at taco stands in Chicago add a hit of acidity and color, I have to include them at the party, as well. My sides are a little Korean, a little American, and a little Latin. I'm still that kid from Chicago, not quite fitting in, but happy to be part of a few cultures with my food.

Kimchi Salsa

In Korea, people make kimchi every fall. It's a big ritual; families bury it in their yard to let it age for a year or even longer. Some people love how funky kimchi gets when it's aged for a long time, but you will never hear me brag about how old my kimchi is. I like bright flavors, so we make the kimchi fresh every day at our restaurants. The secret is the Magic Paste. If you have a tub of it on hand, that means its spicy, garlicky flavors are ready to turn cabbage into kimchi in just a few minutes.

—

1 pound napa cabbage

3 cups water

⅓ cup kosher salt

½ cup thinly sliced white onion

½ cup thinly sliced seedless cucumber

1 cup Magic Paste (page 44)

PREP TIME 30 minutes
COOK TIME 5 minutes
MAKES 1 quart

Separate the napa cabbage leaves and stack them on top of one another. Cut the stem and leaves into 2-inch squares (don't worry—they don't have to be perfect) and place them in a large heatproof bowl.

In a small saucepan, bring the water to a boil, add the salt, and stir until the salt dissolves. Pour the salted water over the cabbage and let sit for 15 minutes. Drain the cabbage in a colander, rinse thoroughly under cold running water, and then drain well.

Combine the cabbage, onion, cucumber, and Magic Paste in a large bowl and toss until evenly mixed. Store the kimchi in an airtight container in the refrigerator until you are ready to serve it, ideally the same day.

KUNG FU IT Kimchi is my kind of condiment. It can be added to a sauce like Korean Pesto (page 46), used to season a stew, or tucked into a sandwich or a wrap as a topping. Don't toss the leftover liquid after you've eaten all of the kimchi. It makes a great brine for pork chops before you put them on the grill.

Cucumber Onion Kimchi

If you can, use Kirby cucumbers for this recipe. They can be harder to find, but I think they are worth the hunt. They have less water, which makes them meatier than conventional cucumbers. If you can't find Kirbys, short Persian cucumbers will work. And if you can't find Persian cucumbers, use a seedless English cucumber. You really taste the essence of cucumber in this kimchi, which is a winner on a hot day.

—

6 or 7 Kirby or Persian cucumbers or 3 English cucumbers, thinly sliced

1 red onion, thinly sliced

1½ cups Nuoc Cham Sauce (page 42)

¼ cup toasted sesame oil

1 tablespoon Korean chili flakes

PREP TIME 15 minutes
FEEDS 6 people

Place the cucumbers and onion in a large bowl, add the Nuoc Cham Sauce, sesame oil, and chili flakes, and toss to mix evenly. Cover and chill until you are ready to serve it, ideally the same day you make it.

Korean Coleslaw

This slaw is full of bold flavors from the Nuoc Cham Sauce, but adding the yogurt keeps the dressing light. It's a perfect accompaniment to a fatty pork chop or steak, in the same way you get slaw with pulled pork or brisket in the South. For a light meal, make this the base for a salad with some grilled chicken on top. Don't toss the slaw with the dressing until you are ready to serve. The slaw and dressing will hold separately in the refrigerator for a couple of days before the vegetables lose their crunch.

—

- 1½ cups Nuoc Cham Sauce (page 42)
- ¼ cup toasted sesame oil
- ½ cup plain Greek yogurt
- 2 tablespoons Korean chili flakes
- 1 tablespoon sambal oelek
- 1 small head red cabbage, thinly sliced
- 2 cups thinly sliced napa cabbage
- 2 carrots, peeled, then thinly sliced
- 1 English cucumber or 3 Kirby or Persian cucumbers, thinly sliced
- 1 cup Garlic Herb Peanuts (page 59)
- ½ cup chopped fresh cilantro
- ¼ cup chopped fresh basil

Whisk together the Nuoc Cham Sauce, sesame oil, yogurt, chili flakes, and sambal oelek in a bowl. Cover and refrigerate until you are ready to dress the slaw.

Combine the red cabbage, napa cabbage, carrots, and cucumbers in a large bowl and toss to mix well. Pour the dressing over the vegetables and toss until the dressing is evenly distributed.

Garnish the slaw with the peanuts, cilantro, and basil and serve.

KUNG FU IT This slaw is all about the crunch factor. If you have Garlic Herb Peanuts on hand, use them in this recipe. But if not, plain dry-roasted peanuts will work well. Thinly slicing your vegetables makes it easier for the dressing to cling to them, and the vegetables will soak in the flavors a lot faster.

PREP TIME 20 minutes
FEEDS 6 people

Pickled Red Onions

This is a quick, crunchy, easy-to-make topper that goes with everything grilled. These onions are terrific on tacos and in wraps; the vinegar adds a bright burst of flavor. You can make a big batch of these onions and store them in a jar or an airtight container in the refrigerator for up to two weeks.

—

2 red onions, thinly sliced

2 tablespoons sugar

1 cup rice vinegar

½ cup sherry vinegar

1 tablespoon Korean chili flakes

1 tablespoon coriander seeds

1 tablespoon kosher salt

PREP TIME 10 minutes
COOK TIME 5 minutes
CHILL TIME 1 hour
FEEDS 6 people

Place the red onions in a large heatproof bowl. Combine the sugar, rice vinegar, sherry vinegar, chili flakes, coriander, and salt in a saucepan and bring to a boil over high heat. As soon as the mixture boils, remove it from the heat and pour through a strainer held over the bowl of onions. Let the onions cool to room temperature, then transfer the onions and the pickling liquid to an airtight container and refrigerate for at least an hour and up to 2 weeks before serving.

Sides

Kimchi Potato Salad

One of the great mysteries for me when I go out to traditional Korean barbecue restaurants in America is that they all serve the same generic mayonnaise-based potato salad that you can find in the deli section of any grocery store in the country. Who said potato salad was a Korean *banchan* (snack or side dish), anyway? I always shake my head when the mayo potato salad hits the table and think that it would be so much better to combine potatoes, which are pretty mild, with kimchi. This recipe is my chance to prove my point!

—

3 pounds small red potatoes, halved

1½ cups Nuoc Cham Sauce (page 42)

1½ cups kimchi, homemade (page 166) or store-bought

¼ cup extra-hot prepared horseradish

1½ cups finely chopped celery

1 cup thinly sliced red onion

½ cup chopped fresh cilantro

PREP TIME 25 minutes
COOK TIME 30 minutes
FEEDS 6 people

Place the potatoes in a large saucepan, add water to cover, and bring to a boil over high heat. Turn down the heat to a simmer, cover, and cook for about 30 minutes, until tender when pierced with a fork. Drain the potatoes and cut them into smaller pieces if you like.

Place the Nuoc Cham Sauce, ½ cup of the kimchi, and the horseradish in a food processor and process for about 1 minute, or until well blended and smooth. Transfer the sauce to a large bowl and stir in the remaining 1 cup kimchi, celery, onion, and cilantro, mixing well. Add the potatoes and toss to coat evenly. Cover and refrigerate until you are ready to eat. It will keep for up to 3 days.

Hoisin Baked Beans with Bacon BBQ Crust

I couldn't stand baked beans until I met my wife, Yvonne. Because she loves beans, I knew I had to figure out a way to enjoy eating them. I don't like their texture (it's too soft for me), so giving baked beans a crunchy crust of bread crumbs and bacon makes both of us happy. This is my twist on a classic American barbecue side dish. I use canned red kidney beans here, but black beans or chickpeas would be good, too.

—

1 pound sliced bacon, finely chopped

2 tablespoons olive oil

2 cups chopped white onion

3 cloves garlic, minced

¼ cup bourbon

■ ¼ cup Soy Balsamic Sauce (page 38)

¼ cup light brown sugar, firmly packed

½ cup water

½ cup hoisin sauce

½ cup ketchup

1 tablespoon Worcestershire sauce

2 tablespoons sambal oelek

4 cups drained canned red kidney beans, rinsed (about three 15-ounce cans)

2 cups panko (Japanese bread crumbs)

■ 2 tablespoons BBQ Spice Rub (page 52)

PREP TIME 30 minutes
COOK TIME 45 minutes
FEEDS 6 people

Heat a large, deep sauté pan over medium heat. Add the bacon and sauté for 5 to 7 minutes, until crispy. Using a slotted spoon, transfer the bacon to paper towels to drain. Remove 2 tablespoons of the bacon fat from the pan and set aside. Add the oil to the pan, then add the onion and garlic and sauté over medium heat until tender, about 3 minutes.

Take the hot pan off the stove, add the bourbon, return the pan to the burner, and scrape up all of the browned bits from the pan bottom with a wooden spoon, then cook until the bourbon has almost evaporated. Add the Soy Balsamic Sauce, brown sugar, water, hoisin sauce, ketchup, Worcestershire sauce, and sambal oelek and stir well. Add half of the cooked bacon and all of the beans to the pan, stir well, and simmer for 3 minutes. Remove from the heat.

To make the crust, put the panko, the remaining cooked bacon, the reserved 2 tablespoons bacon fat, and the spice rub in a food processor and process for about 1 minute, until well blended.

Heat the grill for direct heat cooking to medium (350°F to 375°F), or preheat the oven to 350°F.

Transfer the bean mixture to a baking pan and top evenly with the bread crumb mixture. Place on the grill grate and close the lid, or place in the oven, and cook for about 30 minutes, until the top is a deep brown color. Remove from the grill and serve.

CONTINUED

Hoisin Baked Beans with Bacon BBQ Crust

CONTINUED

KUNG FU IT If you don't want to use bacon in your beans, puree 2 chipotle chilies in adobo sauce with 2 tablespoons of the sauce and add to the sauté pan when you add the beans. The chilies and sauce will give the beans some of the smokiness you would otherwise get from the bacon. You can use 4 tablespoons of olive oil to sauté the onion and garlic in place of the bacon fat in the panko mixture.

Thai Basil Eggplant

This is a take on one of the best-selling side dishes at our restaurants, and with good reason. Eggplant can be very mild, so you don't want to drown it with too much heat. A little bit of sambal oelek goes a long way here, adding plenty of spice, which is balanced nicely by the nutty, smooth sesame oil.

—

■ 1½ cups Nuoc Cham Sauce (page 42)

2 tablespoons sambal oelek

2 tablespoons toasted sesame oil

¼ cup sugar

3 Chinese or Japanese eggplants, halved lengthwise

½ cup olive oil

¼ cup chopped fresh Thai basil

PREP TIME 20 minutes
COOK TIME 4 to 6 minutes
FEEDS 6 people

Heat the grill for direct heat cooking to medium (350°F to 375°F).

Combine the Nuoc Cham Sauce, sambal oelek, sesame oil, and sugar in a small bowl and whisk together until well mixed. Set aside.

Brush the eggplant halves with the oil, place on the grill grate, close the lid, and cook for 2 to 3 minutes. Flip the eggplants over, close the lid, and cook for another 2 to 3 minutes, until browned and tender.

Transfer the eggplants to a cutting board and let cool slightly. Cut crosswise into thin slices and transfer to a large, shallow dish. Pour the sauce over the eggplant and stir to coat evenly. Garnish the eggplant with the basil and serve.

KUNG FU IT You can make a fast and tasty dip with leftover eggplant. Place 1 cup of the eggplant with its sauce in a food processor, add 1 cup drained canned beans (any kind), and process until well blended and smooth. Serve with rice crackers, raw vegetables, or tortilla chips.

Coconut Grits

I like to cook something southern every now and then to remind me of when I worked in Atlanta, and shrimp and grits was one of the dishes I especially enjoyed during my time there. But I've since realized that I am allergic to dairy, and grits are usually laced with tons of cheese, butter, and cream. I have solved the problem of grits and other dairy-rich dishes by replacing any dairy with nondairy alternatives, like tofu cream cheese, coconut milk, and coconut butter. We still use some dairy at our restaurants, but the amount is minimal. I am proud that we can accommodate dairy-averse guests, and doing so encourages us to be creative with how we cook, like with these grits, which get an unexpected jolt of flavor from the coconut milk in this recipe.

——

2 tablespoons olive oil

¼ cup chopped white onion

2 cloves garlic, minced

2 cups water

1 (13½-ounce) can coconut milk

1 cup stone-ground grits, yellow or white

1 teaspoon salt

¼ cup Nuoc Cham Sauce (page 42)

2 tablespoons fish sauce

2 tablespoons sherry vinegar

PREP TIME 20 minutes
COOK TIME 50 minutes
FEEDS 6 people

Heat the grill for direct heat cooking to medium (350°F to 375°F), or preheat the oven to 350°F.

Heat the oil in a large saucepan over medium heat. Add the onion and sauté for 3 minutes, until tender, then add the garlic and sauté for 1 minute. Pour in the water and coconut milk and bring to a simmer. Add the grits and simmer, stirring, until the liquid thickens.

Remove from the heat and cover with foil or an oven-safe lid. Place on the grill grate and close the lid, or place in the oven, and cook for about 45 minutes, until creamy.

Remove from the grill or oven, add the salt, Nuoc Cham Sauce, fish sauce, and vinegar, and stir well, then serve.

Kung Fu Your Leftovers

If there is one thing all Koreans can agree on, it's that we will not throw out leftover food! It goes against my nature to waste food, especially after I have put in the time and care to buy the best products and cook them perfectly. Leftovers are my jam, and the recipes in this chapter are on regular rotation at my house, especially after a Sunday afternoon barbecue when the fridge is full of leftover meats, veggies, and sauces.

So how do you Kung Fu your leftovers? You turn them into dishes that don't resemble the originals but have tons of flavor, texture, style, and personality. This book is no longer about me telling you what to do; it's time for you to take the lead and apply the lessons to your own cooking. Do you love Maryland-style crabs? Then maybe add some Old Bay to the Korean Pesto you put on your grilled crabs. Do you have a jar of *harissa* hanging out in your fridge?

I'll bet it would be a good addition to the Korean Coleslaw (page 170). Need ideas on how to jazz up an omelet or a fried egg? Try a pinch of my Curry Salt (page 50) or some Korean Pesto Butter (see page 157) and see where it takes you. And if your version of Curry Salt includes a little cumin because you love the flavor, that's even better.

Take the master sauces and spice rubs, plus any leftovers and whatever else you have on hand, and create your own dishes from your kitchen, not mine. Make a sandwich, salad, or grains the base and experiment with all of the different ingredients to find your favorite combination. Will you have some bombs? Of course you will. I've made plenty of mediocre or weird plates of food. The whole thing is a learning process, so get out of your head! This is cooking, and that means have fun with it, learn how to do it well, and remember that there aren't a lot of rules.

How to Kung Fu Your Leftover Master Sauces

So you have leftover master sauces in your fridge or freezer? Don't worry—there are dozens of other marinades, salad dressings, dipping sauces, and glazes you can make with one of the master sauces as the base. Think about the flavors already in the sauce and about how you can build on them to create your own version. Here are a few of my favorites to get you started.

KOREAN BBQ SAUCE (PAGE 34)
START WITH ½ CUP LEFTOVER SAUCE AND THEN:

Add ¼ cup *gochujang* to make a spicy BBQ sauce

Add ¼ cup plain Greek yogurt, 1 teaspoon Korean chili flakes, and ½ teaspoon ground cumin to make a tandoori-style marinade

Add ¼ cup bourbon and 1 tablespoon crushed black pepper to make a Korean cowboy marinade

Add ¼ cup plain Greek yogurt and 1 tablespoon Madras curry powder to make Korean-accented tandoori marinade

LEMONGRASS CHILI SAUCE (PAGE 36)
START WITH ½ CUP LEFTOVER SAUCE AND THEN:

Add ¼ cup *gochujang* and 1 tablespoon toasted sesame oil to make a sweet and spicy BBQ sauce

Add ¼ cup bottled yuzu or fresh lime juice and ¼ cup hoisin sauce to make a spicy citrus BBQ sauce

Add 1 ripe avocado, halved, pitted, peeled, and mashed, to make a sandwich spread

KOREAN PESTO (PAGE 46)
START WITH ½ CUP LEFTOVER SAUCE AND THEN:

Add ½ cup store-bought hummus and ¼ cup Nuoc Cham Sauce (page 42) to make a dipping sauce

Add ¼ cup capers and ¼ cup cashews, chopped, to make a sauce

Add 2 tablespoons toasted sesame oil, ¼ cup chopped fresh cilantro, and ¼ cup chopped fresh flat-leaf parsley to make a sesame *chimichurri*

Add 2 tablespoons mayonnaise to make pesto mayonnaise

KO-RICAN SAUCE (PAGE 40)
START WITH ½ CUP LEFTOVER SAUCE AND THEN:

Add ¼ cup pineapple juice and 2 chipolte chilies in adoblo sauce to make an *al pastor* marinade

Add ¼ cup plain Greek yogurt, ¼ cup kimchi (homemade, page 166, or store-bought), and 2 tablespoons Nuoc Cham Sauce (page 42) to make a BBQ marinade

Add ¼ cup fresh orange juice and 2 table-spoons toasted sesame oil to make a zesty Asian dipping sauce or salad dressing

Add ¼ cup water and 2 cups chopped fresh herb leaves of your choice to make a not-your-regular *chimichurri*

NUOC CHAM SAUCE (PAGE 42)
START WITH ½ CUP LEFTOVER SAUCE AND THEN:

Add ¼ cup plain Greek yogurt and 1 tablespoon Korean chili flakes to make Korean *tzatziki* sauce

Add 1 ripe avocado, halved, pitted, peeled, and mashed; ¼ cup plain Greek yogurt; and ¼ cup minced fresh cilantro to make Korean green goddess dressing

Add 2 teaspoons extra-hot prepared horseradish and ¼ cup pureed kimchi (homemade, page 166, or store-bought) to make kimchi Nuoc Cham Sauce

Add 2 tablespoons toasted sesame oil, 1 tablespoon sambal oelek, and 2 tablespoons minced green olives to make a vegetable marinade

Add 1 teaspoon Madras curry powder and ¼ cup mayonnaise to make a curry sandwich spread

Add ½ cup chopped tomato and ¼ cup chopped fresh cilantro to make an Asian pico de gallo

SOY BALSAMIC SAUCE (PAGE 38)
START WITH ½ CUP LEFTOVER SAUCE AND THEN:

Add 2 teaspoons extra-hot prepared horseradish and ¼ cup water to make a Korean sushi dipping sauce

Add ½ teaspoon dried oregano; 1 clove garlic, chopped; and ¼ cup olive oil to make a salad dressing

Add 1 tablespoon Dijon mustard, 2 tablespoons water, and ¼ cup olive oil to make a salad dressing

Add 1 tablespoon red wine and 1 teaspoon ground black pepper to make a tangier, peppery sauce

Add 1 teaspoon chili powder and ¼ cup Lemongrass Chili Sauce (page 36) to make a dipping sauce

Add 2 tablespoons tamarind water, 2 tablespoons tomato paste, and 2 tablespoons brown sugar to make a BBQ dipping sauce (I call this the DJ-Q)

Add ¼ cup coconut milk and ¼ cup DJ-Q (above) to make a coconut BBQ sauce

Add 1 tablespoon hoisin sauce, ¼ cup brandy, and 1 teaspoon chopped fresh rosemary to make a drunken BBQ sauce

Add 1 teaspoon extra-hot prepared horseradish to make a spicy soy sauce

MAGIC PASTE (PAGE 44)
START WITH ½ CUP LEFTOVER SAUCE AND THEN:

Add ¼ cup distilled white vinegar and use as a base for a *lechon* marinade

Add ¼ cup fresh orange juice to make a *mojo* sauce to serve with pork, chicken, or fish

Add ½ cup bourbon and 2 tablespoons *gojuchang* for a spicy pork marinade

Add 4 ripe avocados, halved, pitted, peeled, and mashed, to make guacamole

Kimchi Potluck Stew

When I cook at home, it's usually the lazy man's way of cooking. I cook every day at our restaurants, so at home I want a break! This kimchi stew is perfect for me, because you throw leftovers and everything else in with the broth and in less than a half hour you have something delicious with little effort. Like nearly all stews, this one tastes even better the next day. Also, if you make a big enough batch, it is the perfect stew to stash in your freezer. For an even heartier meal, accompany the stew with rice.

—

8 cups hot water

1 cup doenjang (Korean soybean paste)

2 tablespoons gochujang

2 tablespoons fish sauce

2 tablespoons olive oil

1 yellow onion, coarsely chopped

1 cup sliced white mushrooms

2 cups kimchi, homemade (page 166) or store-bought, chopped

2 cups drained canned hominy, rinsed

1 lime, halved

1 pound leftover raw or cooked meat or seafood, cut into 1-inch pieces

1 pound firm tofu, drained and cut into 1-inch cubes

1 teaspoon cumin seeds

¼ cup chopped fresh cilantro

Pour the hot water into a large bowl and whisk in the doenjang, gochujang, and fish sauce to make a broth.

Heat the oil in a 6-quart stockpot or Dutch oven over medium-high heat. Add the onion, mushrooms, and kimchi and sauté for 3 minutes, until the vegetables are tender. Pour the broth into the pot, add the hominy, lime halves, meat or seafood, and tofu and bring to a simmer. If the meat or seafood is raw, simmer the stew for 20 minutes, until the meat or seafood is cooked through. If the meat is cooked, simmer for only 10 minutes to blend the flavors.

To finish the stew, fish out the lime halves, and when cool enough to handle, squeeze the juice into the stew. Add the cumin seeds, garnish with the cilantro, and serve.

KUNG FU IT If you cannot find *doenjang*, which is a thick fermented soybean paste sold in brown tubs, omit it and swap in 8 cups low-sodium vegetable broth for the water.

PREP TIME 25 minutes
COOK TIME 15 to 25 minutes
FEEDS 6 people

Korean BBQ

Grilled Shrimp Egg Foo Yung

It took me a long time to understand what egg foo yung was or how to cook it, but once I tried it—oh boy! It's like an omelet but done in a wok, and it is a great way to use up leftover vegetables, tofu, and meat. This is the clean-out-your-fridge stir-fry of Korean BBQ.

—

¼ cup olive oil

4 eggs, lightly beaten

1 cup thinly sliced green cabbage

¼ cup thinly sliced green onions, white and green parts

2 handfuls bean sprouts

1 clove garlic, minced

2 pounds leftover Seoul to Buffalo Shrimp (page 126)

1 pound firm tofu, drained and diced

1 tablespoon Korean chili flakes

¼ cup Nuoc Cham Sauce (page 42)

1 teaspoon Curry Salt (page 50)

Lettuce cups or cooked rice or noodles, for serving

PREP TIME 10 minutes
COOK TIME 4 minutes
FEEDS 6 people

Heat the oil in a wok or sauté pan over high heat until hot. Pour the eggs directly onto the oil, mix vigorously for 2 minutes, until the eggs just start to cook, and then add the cabbage, green onions, bean sprouts, garlic, shrimp, tofu, and chili flakes and cook, stirring, for 2 minutes, until the eggs are barely set, like soft scrambled eggs. Stir in the Nuoc Cham Sauce and Curry Salt.

Transfer the stir-fry to a serving dish. To eat, spoon into the lettuce cups or serve over rice or tossed with noodles.

Chicken and Corn Salad

We usually have a lot of leftover cooked chicken around the house, which means we have to come up with new recipes to use it up. Sometimes on Sundays, we grill chicken marinated in Ko-Rican Sauce (page 40) and corn on the cob. We like to make salad the next day with the leftovers and some tortilla chips. It's a lazy—but tasty!—way to start the week.

—

½ cup plain Greek yogurt

2 tablespoons toasted sesame oil

■ ½ cup Nuoc Cham Sauce (page 42)

4 cups (about 2 pounds) leftover cooked chicken, sliced or shredded

Kernels from 2 ears grilled corn (plain or leftover from Korean Elotes, page 160)

3 celery stalks, thinly sliced

¼ cup thinly sliced red onion

1 cup thinly sliced seedless cucumber

4 fresh basil leaves, thinly sliced

2 cups tortilla chips

Combine the yogurt, oil, and Nuoc Cham Sauce in a small bowl and whisk together, mixing well.

Place the chicken, corn kernels, celery, onion, cucumber, basil, and tortilla chips in a large bowl and toss to combine. Pour half of the dressing over the salad and toss gently, coating all of the ingredients evenly, then taste and adjust with more of the dressing if you like.

NOTE If you are saving this salad to eat over a couple of days, don't add the tortilla chips until you are ready to serve it. That way they won't get soggy. It is easy to portion the chips and mix them in according to how much of the salad you are eating each time.

PREP TIME 20 minutes
FEEDS 6 people

Korean BBQ

Salad Matrix

START WITH A CRISP, REFRESHING BASE	+	ADD SOMETHING HEARTY	+	THROW IN SOMETHING HEALTHY
arugula		boiled baby potatoes		diced avocado
iceberg lettuce		canned beans		cubed Blackened BBQ Tofu (page 146)
shredded raw cabbage		leftover noodles		Garlic Herb Peanuts (page 59)
mixed salad greens		sliced mushrooms		leftover quinoa
spinach		crumbled hard-boiled eggs		leftover wild rice
chopped romaine lettuce		bacon		
		crumbled blue cheese		

The day after a big barbecue, I like to go a little lighter with a salad. These ones hit the spot.

CHICKEN BLT SALAD

romaine lettuce
+
bacon
+
avocado
+
tomatoes
+
Lemongrass Chicken
+
Korean Pesto

BBQ PORK SALAD

cabbage
+
canned beans
+
Garlic Herb Peanuts
+
carrots
+
Korean al Pastor
+
Ko-Rican Sauce

+ TOP WITH VEGETABLES	**+ ADD A LEFTOVER PROTEIN PUNCH**	**+ FINISH WITH A DRESSING**
diced tomatoes	crumbled Curried Chicken Burger patties (page 117)	Korean Pesto (page 46)
diced bell peppers	Seoul to Buffalo Shrimp (page 126)	Ko-Rican Sauce (page 40)
broccoli florets, raw or cooked	Sesame Hoisin Chicken Wings (page 113)	Nuoc Cham Sauce (page 42)
Gochujang Asparagus (page 155)	Korean BBQ Salmon (page 129)	Soy Balsamic Sauce (page 38)
blanched green beans	Korean BBQ Skirt Steak (page 82)	
thinly sliced carrots	Lemongrass Chicken (page 110)	
sliced cucumber	Korean al Pastor (page 89)	
	Spicy Lemongrass Squid (page 139)	

SPINACH SALMON SALAD	**STEAK SALAD**	**SQUID SALAD**
spinach	arugula	mixed salad greens
+	+	+
bacon	blue cheese	mushrooms
+	+	+
avocado	avocado	avocado
+	+	+
Gochujang Asparagus	tomatoes	tomatoes
+	+	+
Korean BBQ Salmon	Korean BBQ Skirt Steak	Spicy Lemongrass Squid
+	+	+
Nuoc Cham Sauce	Ko-Rican Sauce	Soy Balsamic Sauce

Grilled Cauliflower and Soba Noodle Salad

To me, soba noodles are better cold than hot. The noodles have their own flavor, but what's great is that they will also take on the flavors of the pesto sauce in this recipe. I especially like the combination of basil and soba. This dish is in heavy rotation in our house; it's just so easy to make.

—

Kosher salt

8 ounces dried soba noodles

2 tablespoons vegetable oil

2 leftover Cauliflower Steaks with Korean Pesto (page 151), roughly chopped

1 pint cherry tomatoes, halved

1 bunch radishes, thinly sliced

■ 1 cup Korean Pesto (page 46)

Bring a large pot of water to a boil over high heat and season it with salt. Add the noodles and cook for about 6 minutes, until tender but not mushy. Drain and rinse under cold running water, then toss them in the vegetable oil and refrigerate about 30 minutes, until chilled.

Place the cauliflower, tomatoes, radishes, and pesto in a large bowl and toss together gently until well mixed. Add the cold noodles, toss again gently, and serve.

PREP TIME 10 minutes
COOK TIME 10 minutes
CHILL TIME 30 minutes
FEEDS 6 people

Al Pastor Pork Quinoa Bowl with Korean Pesto Tomatoes

My wife Yvonne adores quinoa, which is lucky because she is gluten intolerant and can't eat most pasta salads. But there is no way she is going to eat the bland quinoa salads you see out there—remember, she is the fiery Puerto Rican half of our Ko-Rican team, and does not do boring food. So I created this quinoa salad for her, full with the flavor of Korean Pesto and leftover Korean al Pastor.

—

2¾ cups water

1½ cups quinoa, rinsed

¼ teaspoon kosher salt

■ 1 cup Korean Pesto (page 46)

2 tomatoes, chopped

¼ cup coarsely torn fresh mint leaves

1 cup bean sprouts

2 pounds leftover Korean al Pastor (page 89) or any leftover meat or tofu

PREP TIME 25 minutes
COOK TIME 20 minutes
FEEDS 6 people

Combine the water, quinoa, and salt in a saucepan and bring to a boil over medium-high heat. Reduce the heat to a gentle simmer, cover, and cook for 15 minutes. Remove from the heat and let rest for 5 minutes, then fluff the quinoa with a fork.

Place the pesto, tomatoes, mint, and bean sprouts in a large bowl and toss until the vegetables are evenly coated with the pesto. Add the quinoa and toss again until mixed.

Warm the pork in a preheated 400°F oven or in a sauté pan over low heat for 5 minutes, then place on top of the quinoa salad and serve.

Bowl Matrix

START WITH LEFTOVER PROTEIN IN ⅓ OF THE BOWL	+	SPOON IN LEFTOVER GRAINS TO ⅓ OF THE BOWL	+	ADD EXTRA SUBSTANCE TO ⅓ OF THE BOWL
chicken		wheat berries		leftover rice noodles
pork		farro		leftover soba noodles
Korean BBQ Skirt Steak (page 82)		bulgur		arugula
Blackened BBQ Tofu (page 146)		quinoa		coarsely chopped romaine lettuce
canned black beans		freekeh		leftover couscous
Seoul to Buffalo Shrimp (page 126)		rice		leftover orzo
salmon or trout		barley		sliced tortillas
Lola's Thanksgiving Turkey (page 109)		buckwheat		pita chips

The easiest way to turn your leftovers into something new is to simply empty them into a bowl and mix them up. Here's how I do it.

TOFU BREAKFAST BOWL

Blackened BBQ Tofu
+
quinoa
+
arugula
+
Lemongrass Chili Sauce
+
sautéed bok choy
+
fried egg

TURKEY SALAD BOWL

Lola's Thanksgiving Turkey
+
quinoa
+
soba noodles
+
Korean BBQ Sauce
+
green beans
+
green onions & cilantro

DRIZZLE WITH A MASTER SAUCE	TUCK IN SOME VEGETABLES	GARNISH FOR EXTRA FLAVOR
Korean Pesto (page 46)	**Gochujang Asparagus (page 155)**	**basil**
Nuoc Cham Sauce (page 42)	**raw sliced cabbage**	**cilantro**
Soy Balsamic Sauce (page 38)	**sliced red and green peppers**	**Korean chili flakes**
Ko-Rican Sauce (page 40)	**sautéed bok choy**	**yuzu juice**
Lemongrass Chili Sauce (page 36)	**shelled edamame**	**lemon juice**
Korean BBQ Sauce (page 34)	**shredded carrots**	**dill**
Korean tzatziki sauce (see page 185)	**avocado**	**green onions**
	Pickled Red Onions (page 173)	**fried egg**
	blanched green beans	**Garlic Herb Peanuts (page 59)**

GREEK STEAK SANDWICH BOWL

Korean BBQ Skirt Steak

+

buckwheat

+

orzo & pita chips

+

Korean tzatziki sauce

+

Pickled Red Onions

+

Garlic Herb Peanuts & basil

KOREAN SHRIMP TACO BOWL

Seoul to Buffalo Shrimp

+

farro

+

tortillas

+

Ko-Rican Sauce

+

avocado

+

green onions

BEEF AND ASPARAGUS BOWL

Korean BBQ Skirt Steak

+

wheat berries

+

soba noodles

+

Korean BBQ Sauce

+

Gochujang Asparagus

+

basil

Stir-Fried Soy Balsamic Portabello Mushrooms with Long-Life Noodles

If you have a large cast-iron skillet, use it for this quick stir-fry dish. It is an easy, one-pot supper I like to make when I want to relax and enjoy my food without having to do a lot of work to get it on the table. I like to eat this on New Year's Day, when I don't feel like cooking much but want to follow the tradition of eating noodles for long life and good luck for the year. At my house, no forks are allowed with this stir-fry. Instead, we use chopsticks, the perfect tool for tasting everything in one bite.

———

¼ cup olive oil

3 eggs, lightly beaten

1 yellow onion, thinly sliced

1 cup coarsely chopped asparagus

3 leftover Sizzling Soy Balsamic Portabello Mushrooms (page 149), sliced

2 cups chopped arugula or romaine lettuce

3 (10-ounce) packages precooked Japanese udon noodles (thick wheat noodles)

½ cup coconut milk

■ ½ cup Korean Pesto (page 46)

Heat the oil in a large cast-iron skillet or sauté pan over high heat until hot. Pour the eggs directly into the oil, mix vigorously for 2 minutes, until the eggs just start to cook, and then add the onion and cook, stirring, for 1 minute. Add the asparagus, mushrooms, and arugula and cook, stirring, for 3 minutes, until the vegetables are tender. Add the udon and then the coconut milk and pesto, stir everything together, and let reduce for about 2 minutes, until the sauce thickly coats the udon.

Transfer to a large serving platter and serve.

PREP TIME 30 minutes
COOK TIME 10 minutes
FEEDS 6 people

Korean BBQ

Mixed Veggie Stir-Fry

The idea here is to use it all—whatever you have left over—whether vegetables, seafood, or meat. Every country has a dish like this one, but because everyone's leftovers are always changing, no two dishes are ever alike. If you don't have enough leftovers, do what we cooks do when we don't know how to finish a dish: put a fried egg on top to make it extra satisfying.

—

2 slices bacon

2 tablespoons olive oil

2 eggs, lightly beaten

½ cup coarsely chopped leftover Cauliflower Steaks with Korean Pesto (page 151)

½ cup coarsely chopped leftover Gochujang Asparagus (page 155)

1 cup coarsely chopped green cabbage

■ 2 tablespoons Korean Pesto (page 46)

PREP TIME 30 minutes
COOK TIME 6 minutes
FEEDS 2 people

Place a grill pan on the grill, then heat the grill for direct heat cooking to medium-high (400°F to 450°F).

Place the bacon in the grill pan and cook, turning once, for 2 minutes on each side, until crisp and browned. Remove the bacon from the pan, leaving the bacon fat, and cut the bacon into pieces. Pour the oil into the pan with the bacon fat, then pour the eggs directly into the oil and mix vigorously for 2 minutes, until the eggs just start to cook. Add the cauliflower, asparagus, and cabbage and cook for 2 more minutes, stirring frequently, until the cabbage wilts and the eggs are set. Mix in the pesto and serve.

KUNG FU IT Is this your morning-after-the-barbecue hangover breakfast? Then just make this on the stove in your pj's and eat it in bed.

Blackened Tofu Lettuce Wraps

This recipe is like a lettuce taco. It has a protein, sauce, and vegetables and it is a fresh and healthy way to eat up your leftovers. Perilla leaves have a green, herbal flavor and are sold in Asian grocery stores. If you cannot find them, Bibb lettuce or shiso leaves are a good substitute.

—

6 green onions, trimmed, cut into 4 pieces each

2 tablespoons olive oil

2 teaspoons Curry Salt (page 50)

24 sesame (perilla) leaves or Bibb lettuce leaves

3 cups (1 pound) leftover cubed Blackened BBQ Tofu with marinade (page 146)

1 (15-ounce) can black beans, drained

2 cups arugula

24 cilantro sprigs

PREP TIME 30 minutes
FEEDS 6 people

Place the green onions in a large bowl, drizzle with the oil, and toss to coat evenly. Sprinkle with the Curry Salt, toss again, and set aside for 5 minutes. Sear them in a very hot pan if you like, or skip this step if you don't feel like cooking anything.

Line up the sesame leaves in a single layer on large serving platters or trays. Top the leaves with the tofu, then with the green onions, black beans, arugula, and cilantro, and lastly with the leftover tofu marinade, dividing each ingredient evenly, then serve. I sometimes eat these wraps while standing over my sink to eliminate the mess.

Kung Fu Your Leftovers

Sandwich Matrix

START WITH A WRAPPER	+	SMEAR ON A SAUCE OR SPREAD	+	ADD SOME VEGETABLES FOR CRISP CRUNCH
bread		mayonnaise flavored with a master sauce or spice rub		Gochujang Asparagus (page 155)
pita bread		Seoulthern Pimento Cheese (page 66)		Sizzling Soy Balsamic Portabello Mushrooms (page 149)
bao buns		Dijon mustard		grilled green onions
lettuce leaves		Korean Pesto (page 46)		arugula
corn or flour tortillas		gochujang		Kimchi, homemade (page 166) or store-bought
		Soy Balsamic Sauce (page 38)		Pickled Red Onions (page 173)
		Korean Baba Ghanoush (page 65)		lettuce leaves
		Korean tzatziki sauce (see page 185)		tomato slices
		Magic Paste guacamole (see page 185)		Garlic Herb Peanuts (page 59)
		Edamame Hummus (page 61)		crushed lentil chips

I've been a pile-it-high sandwich guy since I was a kid. Here are a few favorites made with leftovers.

SALMON AVOCADO TOAST

baguette
+
Magic Paste guacamole
+
tomato slices
+
crushed lentil chips
+
Korean BBQ Salmon

AL PASTOR EGG SANDWICH

baguette
+
Korean Pesto
+
Gochujang Asparagus
+
sunny-side up fried egg &
Korean al Pastor

+ **PICK A MEAT OR OTHER PROTEIN**

Blackened BBQ Tofu (page 146)

Korean BBQ Skirt Steak (page 82)

Korean al Pastor (page 89)

Lemongrass Chicken (page 110)

Lola's Thanksgiving Turkey (page 109)

Korean BBQ Salmon (page 129)

sunny-side up fried egg

TOFU BUN

bao buns

+

mayonnaise

+

Pickled Red Onions

+

Blackened BBQ Tofu

TURKEY TACO

corn tortillas

+

Edamame Hummus

+

lettuce

+

Lola's Thanksgiving Turkey

CHICKEN SALAD SANDWICH

baguette

+

Soy Balsamic Sauce & Dijon mustard

+

lettuce

+

Lemongrass Chicken

Kung Fu Your Leftovers

Korean BBQ Skirt Steak Tacos

I always grill extra Korean BBQ Skirt Steak so I can make tacos with the leftovers at least once a week. This version reminds me of carne asada tacos, one of the greatest things to eat on vacation. You'll want an ice-cold beer to drink with these.

½ cup coarsely chopped kimchi, homemade (page 166) or store-bought

1 cup chopped tomato

¼ cup Nuoc Cham Sauce (page 42)

1 ripe avocado, halved, pitted, peeled, and chopped

1 tablespoon sambal oelek

12 (6-inch) corn tortillas

2 pounds leftover Korean BBQ Skirt Steak (page 82)

1 cup Pickled Red Onions (page 173)

¼ cup coarsely chopped fresh cilantro

PREP TIME 20 minutes
COOK TIME 8 minutes
FEEDS 6 people

Place the kimchi, tomato, Nuoc Cham Sauce, avocado, and sambal oelek in a bowl and toss together, mixing well.

Heat a sauté pan over high heat. In batches, heat the tortillas in the hot pan for about 20 seconds on each side, until warm and pliable. Stack them as you heat them, then wrap the stack in aluminum foil until everything is ready.

Warm the steak in a large sauté pan over low heat for 5 minutes.

Everyone is in charge of assembling his or her own tacos: Place 2 warm tortillas on a plate, top each with the skirt steak, followed by a spoonful of the kimchi tomato salsa, and then the pickled onions and cilantro to finish.

Korean Kitchen Sink Pasta Salad

This dish is simple, summery, and quick. It's great for a large party or to take to a picnic, and you can make plenty of it without spending hours in the kitchen. I like to put small amounts of pasta salad into lettuce cups so it's easy for people to grab and looks neat and clean on the table.

———

3 tablespoons kosher salt

1 pound penne pasta

■ 1 cup Nuoc Cham Sauce (page 42)

¼ cup toasted sesame oil

1½ pounds leftover Korean BBQ Skirt Steak (page 82), cut into bite-size pieces

¼ cup thinly sliced red onion

1 pint cherry tomatoes, halved

8 ounces firm tofu, drained and cut into small cubes

2 ripe avocados, halved, pitted, peeled, and diced

½ cup pitted green olives, sliced

¼ cup loosely packed fresh basil leaves, coarsely chopped

1 cup dry-roasted peanuts, chopped

Lettuce cups, for serving

Bring a large pot of water to a boil and add the salt. Add the pasta and cook for about 10 minutes (or according to package directions), until al dente. Drain and rinse under cold running water.

Whisk together the Nuoc Cham Sauce and sesame oil in a large bowl. Add the steak, onion, tomatoes, tofu, avocado, pasta, olives, basil, and peanuts and toss well. Cover and refrigerate about 30 minutes, until chilled, then spoon into lettuce cups to serve.

KUNG FU IT There is a lot in this pasta salad, so feel free to skip the steak or tofu if you don't have it on hand. Pasta salad is flexible, and you should be, too. Use any kind of pasta you have sitting around for this salad—even noodles or lasagna sheets broken into pieces. Feel free to clean out your pantry for this kitchen sink dish.

PREP TIME 30 minutes
COOK TIME 15 minutes
CHILL TIME 30 minutes
FEEDS 6 to 8 people

Kung Fu Your Leftovers

Pesto Matrix

START WITH 1 CUP OF FRESH LEAVES FROM AN HERB (OR TWO) IN A FOOD PROCESSOR	+ ADD ¼ CUP NUTS	+ BLEND IN ¼ CUP OF SALTY, FLAVORFUL INGREDIENTS
basil	dry-roasted peanuts	Thai curry paste
Thai basil	cashews	Nuoc Cham Sauce (page 42) or fish sauce
cilantro	walnuts	Kimchi, homemade (page 166) or store-bought
flat-leaf parsley	pecans	tamarind
curly parsley	pine nuts	chipotle chilies in adobo sauce
mint	hazelnuts	sun-dried tomatoes
shiso leaves	almonds	olives
arugula	pistachios	capers
		dill pickles

Making your own pesto is easy and is a great way to use up leftover nuts, herbs, and sauces. Here are some ideas to get you started.

CILANTRO PESTO

cilantro
+
cashews
+
kimchi
+
chili oil

THREE HERB PESTO

Thai basil, cilantro & curly parsley
+
pecans
+
dill pickles
+
toasted sesame oil

+ **WHILE THE BLENDER IS RUNNING, ADD ¼ CUP OF OIL**

olive oil

toasted sesame oil

almond oil

chili oil

hazelnut oil

lemon oil

avocado oil

SUGGESTIONS FOR USING YOUR PESTO

• Mix with mayo for a sandwich spread

• Add a spoonful to broth to make a flavorful soup

• Stir into hummus for a dip

• Whisk with oil to make a vinaigrette-style dressing

• Swirl with Greek yogurt to make a sauce

SHISO PESTO

shiso leaves
+
almonds
+
fish sauce
+
almond oil

ARUGULA PESTO

arugula
+
pistachios
+
sun-dried tomatoes
+
olive oil

MINT PESTO

mint
+
pine nuts
+
capers
+
avocado oil

Kung Fu Your Leftovers

Sweet Stuff

I don't have a huge sweet tooth, but I do like a little bite of dessert after a meal, especially after a barbecue with a lot of salty, savory flavors. In summer, I like to serve fruit desserts. They are sweet enough to satisfy a sugar craving, but their acidity is similar to what you taste in some marinades and grilling sauces, so there is a natural flavor transition from the savory part of the meal to dessert. Also, lots of fruits are in season when I am grilling the most, so I make it a point of going to the local farmers' market to see what stone fruits are available for grilling to caramelized perfection or for freezing or pureeing into a light final course. Of course, for many people, it isn't dessert unless it is rich, preferably with chocolate, but I still like to keep even chocolate desserts light.

Regardless of whether you go for something fruity or chocolaty, my rules for dessert are similar to my rules for snacks: First, they should be dishes you can make in advance so you aren't scrambling to put them together while you are grilling the rest of the meal. Second, since you've probably just eaten some snacks, vegetables, meat or seafood, and sides, they should be light and refreshing. You don't want your dessert to kill the party by filling your guests up so much that they want to go home and crash on the sofa! With dessert, you are done cooking and deserve to spend some time around the table, hanging out with family and friends and telling stories. Relax—you've earned it!

Vietnamese Coffee Affogato

I am crazy about coffee of any kind, brewed strong and with a little raw sugar. I don't take milk, half-and-half, or cream, as I want to appreciate the pure flavor of the coffee. But at our restaurants, we serve hot and cold Vietnamese coffee with condensed milk. People love it, even more when we offer the Asian version of an *affogato*, the classic Italian dessert of hot espresso poured over vanilla gelato. I usually use coffee from a local roaster for this recipe, but if you don't have a favorite, use Café Du Monde brand from New Orleans. It has chicory in it, which gives it an extra jolt of gentle bitterness that is a nice contrast with the sweetened condensed milk and ice cream. This is one of the simplest desserts you can make, but it's impressive and memorable.

—

3 cups water

¾ cup coarse-ground dark-roast coffee

¾ cup sweetened condensed milk

4 scoops ice cream (vanilla, chocolate, cinnamon, or mocha)

PREP TIME 4 minutes
FEEDS 4 people

Bring the water to a boil in a small saucepan, add the ground coffee, and remove from the heat. Let steep for 4 minutes.

Pour the steeped coffee through a coffee filter into a pitcher and stir in the condensed milk. Place a scoop of ice cream in each individual dish and pour the hot coffee over the ice cream at the table.

KUNG FU IT You can make this dessert anywhere you go. Brew the coffee on the grill after you've cooked the main course, stir in a can of sweetened condensed milk, and flag down the ice cream truck to buy scoops of ice cream or even ice cream sandwiches to use as the base for the dessert. See? Dessert on the go!

Coconut Chocolate Pudding

One of the sous chefs at bellyQ came up with this recipe, and it is a winner. Sometimes when if I'm in the kitchen by myself first thing in the morning, I will toast a steamed Chinese bao bun, scoop a little of the pudding onto it, and eat it as my secret breakfast.

—

12 ounces semisweet chocolate, chopped

2 (13½-ounce) cans coconut milk

¼ cup sugar

2 teaspoons ground cinnamon

PREP TIME 5 minutes
COOK TIME 10 minutes
CHILL TIME 3 hours
FEEDS 6 people

Place the chocolate in a heatproof bowl. Combine the coconut milk, sugar, and cinnamon in a saucepan and bring to a simmer over medium heat. Cook, stirring often, for 4 minutes. Remove from the heat, pour over the chocolate, and then whisk until the chocolate is melted.

Scrape the pudding into a serving container, cover, and refrigerate for 3 hours, until well chilled and set. Serve chilled.

KUNG FU IT Want a little extra kick? Whisk 3 tablespoons of *gochujang* into the coconut milk mixture. It's a nice complement to the cinnamon, and it gives the chocolate a little spice without overwhelming the flavors.

Sweet Stuff

Mango Lime Frozen Yogurt

This dessert is my take on what my coauthor, Chandra, says her mom used to serve for dessert after Indian dinner parties, and it is also similar to the mango-yogurt smoothies my wife, Yvonne, makes for me in the mornings. The sweet mango puree is a nice balance to the tart, tangy Greek yogurt. No one feels guilty after eating this dessert!

—

2 pints frozen plain Greek yogurt

1 cup canned Kesar mango pulp (I prefer Swad brand)

½ teaspoon grated lime zest

½ cup shaved dried coconut, toasted

PREP TIME 5 minutes
FREEZE TIME 4 hours
FEEDS 6 people

Pull the frozen yogurt from the freezer and let it soften slightly. Place the frozen yogurt and mango puree in a bowl and mix with a rubber spatula until well combined. Quickly return the mixture to the freezer and freeze for at least 4 hours, until firm.

Serve the frozen yogurt garnished with the lime zest and coconut.

Strawberry and Vanilla Yogurt Cheesecake

This dessert isn't even remotely Korean, but it is one I regularly make in the summer, which is the best time to buy strawberries. Even people who say they don't eat dessert, like my wife, will make an exception for this cheesecake. When you are at the farmers' market, pick out the smaller, brightly colored strawberries. They have the best flavor and tend to be sweet, not tart.

—

CRUST

1¼ cups graham cracker crumbs

¼ cup sugar

⅓ cup unsalted butter, melted and cooled

FILLING

2 tablespoons gelatin powder

2 tablespoons hot water

1 cup plain Greek yogurt

6 tablespoons sugar

2 tablespoons plus 1 teaspoon fresh lemon juice

2 teaspoons vanilla extract

Grated zest of 1 lemon

8 ounces cream cheese or tofu cream cheese, at room temperature

1 pint strawberries, hulled and halved

PREP TIME 20 minutes
COOK TIME 8 minutes
CHILL TIME 3 hours
FEEDS 6 people

To make the crust, preheat the oven to 350°F. In a small bowl, stir together the graham cracker crumbs, sugar, and butter until well mixed and evenly moistened. Press the crumb mixture evenly onto the bottom of a 9-inch pie pan.

Bake for about 8 minutes, until lightly browned. Remove from the oven and let cool until you are ready to fill it.

To make the filling, combine the gelatin powder and water in a bowl, whisk together, and then set aside for 3 to 5 minutes, until the gelatin hydrates and softens. Place the yogurt, sugar, lemon juice, and vanilla in a food processor and process for about 1 minute, until smooth. Add the lemon zest and cream cheese and process for 1 more minute, until smooth. Transfer to a large bowl, add the gelatin water, and stir well.

Pour the filling into the cooled crust, cover, and refrigerate for at least 3 hours, until set. Garnish the cheesecake with the strawberries just before serving.

Asian Sangria Float

I was inspired to make this dessert one day while I was working near a Spanish restaurant and watching tables filled with people drinking red wine sangria by the pitcher. Sangria is sweet and fruity, making it already perfect for dessert, so I thought why not create an Asian version? The combination of tropical fruit, wine, and ice cream is great on a hot summer night.

—

1 (750 ml) bottle Sauvignon Blanc or other white wine with bright, citrus flavors

½ cup brandy

½ cup triple sec

¼ cup sugar

¼ cup bottled yuzu or fresh lemon juice

1 cup diced mango

1 orange, cut into thin rounds

1 lime, cut into thin rounds

1 Asian pear or Granny Smith apple, cored and diced

1 pineapple, peeled, cored, and diced

2 cups sparkling water

1 quart vanilla ice cream

Combine the wine, brandy, triple sec, and sugar in a large pitcher or a bowl and stir until the sugar dissolves. Add the yuzu juice, mango, orange and lime slices, pear, and pineapple and stir well. Cover and refrigerate for at least 2 hours or preferably overnight.

Freeze mugs or glasses for 2 hours. Combine the sangria and sparkling water in a pitcher. Scoop ice cream into each mug and pour the sangria (without the fruit) on top. Garnish each serving with fruit from the sangria and serve.

PREP TIME 30 minutes
CHILL TIME 2 to 12 hours
FEEDS 6 people

Grilled Peaches with Cardamom Crepes

Ever since my days as a cook in Atlanta, peaches have been a must for me. There's nothing better than good ol' sun-ripened, peak-of-season juicy peaches. I like to grill them to caramelize their natural sugars.

—

CREPES

1 cup all-purpose flour

1 teaspoon ground cardamom

2 eggs

½ cup whole milk

½ cup water

1 tablespoon honey

¼ teaspoon kosher salt

2 tablespoons unsalted butter, melted

4 ripe peaches, halved and pitted

2 tablespoons vegetable oil

3 tablespoons unsalted butter

¼ cup fresh orange juice

2 tablespoons light brown sugar

1 tablespoon peeled and minced fresh ginger

1 pint fresh blueberries

PREP TIME 15 minutes
COOK TIME 25 minutes
FEEDS 6 people

To make the crepes, whisk together the flour and cardamom in a bowl. Whisk in the eggs and then whisk in the milk, water, and honey. Add the salt and butter and whisk until the batter is lump-free.

Heat an 8-inch nonstick skillet over medium-high heat. Pour ¼ cup of the batter into the pan and immediately tilt and swirl the pan so the batter spreads evenly over the bottom. Cook the crepe for 1 minute, until set. Loosen the edges with a rubber spatula, flip the crepe over, and cook on the other side for 30 seconds, then slide the crepe out of the skillet. Repeat with the remaining batter, stacking the crepes between pieces of waxed or parchment paper. You should have at least 12 crepes.

Heat the grill for indirect heat cooking to medium-high (400°F to 450°F). (If using a charcoal grill, rake the coals to one side of the charcoal grate; if using a gas grill, turn off half of the burners.)

Place the peaches in a bowl, drizzle with the oil, and toss gently to coat evenly. Place the peaches on the grill grate over direct heat and cook for 3 to 4 minutes, until they are somewhat softened and have grill marks. Flip the peaches over away from the heat and cook for another 4 minutes, until the skins blister and start to come off the peaches.

Transfer the peaches to a cutting board and thinly slice them. Melt the butter in a saucepan over medium-high heat, add the orange juice, brown sugar, and ginger, and cook, stirring, for 1 minute. Add the blueberries and peaches and heat until warmed through.

To serve, fold the crepes into quarters, put on plates, and pour the warm peach mixture over the top.

KUNG FU IT If you don't feel like making crepes, pick up some vanilla pound cake or ice cream to serve with the warm fruit.

221

Grilled Pineapple, Mint, and Coconut Popsicles

My brother and I made Popsicles when we were kids, and we would fight over who would get to pick the flavor: fruit punch, grape, or orange. (If I won, it was fruit punch.) This recipe takes me back to those summer afternoons, pretending to be a mad scientist creating things.

—

1 pineapple

2 tablespoons vegetable oil

1 (13½-ounce) can coconut milk

1 cup coconut water

½ cup pure maple syrup

Finely chopped zest of 1 lemon

¼ cup chopped fresh mint

PREP TIME 15 minutes
COOK TIME 10 minutes
FREEZE TIME 4 hours
FEEDS 6 people

Heat the grill for direct heat cooking to medium-high (400°F to 450°F).

Trim the top and bottom off the pineapple, then cut away the skin. Cut the pineapple in half lengthwise, then cut it crosswise into half-moons about ½ inch thick. Place the pineapple in a large bowl, drizzle with the oil, and toss to coat.

Place the pineapple on the grill grate and cook for 4 minutes, until etched with grill marks. Flip the pineapple over and grill on the second side for another 4 minutes, until etched with grill marks. Transfer the pineapple to a cutting board, let sit until cool enough to handle, and then chop into small pieces, discarding any core pieces.

Combine the coconut milk, coconut water, and maple syrup in a saucepan over medium heat on the stove or the grill and heat, stirring occasionally, until the syrup dissolves. Remove from the heat, let cool to room temperature, and then stir in the lemon zest and mint.

Divide the grilled pineapple pieces evenly among 6 Popsicle molds, then fill each mold with the coconut milk mixture. Cover the molds, insert the handles, and freeze for at least 4 hours, until firm.

To serve, fill a container as tall as the molds with hot water, dip the molds briefly in the water just until the pops loosen, and then pull the Popsicles from the molds.

KUNG FU IT Don't have Popsicle molds? You can make mini Popsicles using small plastic cups. Fill them with the pineapple and the coconut milk mixture, cover tightly with plastic wrap, cut a small hole in each covering, stick a wooden Popsicle stick through the hole, and then freeze.

Acknowledgments

From Bill

Let's start by saying thank you to the Dream Team!

YVONNE My wife is my rock. With every new idea or recipe, and whenever I am tasting things, I ask Yvonne her opinion. And when she says, "Do you really want the truth?" I know what that means! She is the one who pushes me, who says, "Go for it!" She is my number one support for anything that I do. Thank you, my lover!

CHANDRA RAM My partner in crime! Thank you for your tireless work on this book. My wife, Chandra, and I share a magical connection— we all have the same birthday, which is a little crazy! Thanks for your insights and for sharing your memories. You made it happen.

CONNIE AND KIKI The recipe angels. Thank you for joining us on this journey. You ladies are incredibly talented and hardworking. I cherish our friendship, and I loved spending time together testing recipes.

JOHNNY AUTRY Our photographer. Thank you for bringing the recipes to life with your images, and for not being afraid to get into the fire. And thank you to your assistant, Nick Erway,

who was a huge help, and ate more vegan noodle bowls than I've ever seen!

AMY COLLINS Thank you for believing in the ideas, for supporting something different, for having the vision, and for seeing things through. I have so much respect for you and your work.

DAD AND MOM You always kept me grounded! We are what others call the American dream. I always tell people that I am from a family of dry cleaners, because that's what my parents did for thirty years. I was lucky that they gave me the freedom to pick what I wanted to do and did not judge me by what I did for a living. Instead, they asked me if I was happy and learning. Without their blessing, I wouldn't have had the courage to do what I do.

MY BROTHER, MIKE; HIS WIFE, JIN; AND MY NEPHEWS, ALEX, DREW, AND MAX I came back to Chicago to spend more time with you, and you gave me a fresh perspective on life. It's not always about the "grand cuisine," as I thought when I was a young cook. It is also about having work-life balance, which I still need to work at! Yes, I still miss birthdays, basketball games, and soccer practices, but I think about you guys often and am proud to talk about you with guests at our restaurants. Thank you for all your love and support.

LOLA, MY MOTHER-IN-LAW, AND YASMINA AND AMANDA, MY SISTERS-IN-LAW Dolores, you have changed how I cook! You have taught me how to season with Latin ingredients and cook with plantains and have taught me recipes that I never would have thought about using. Lastly, thank you for making Yvonne and me so many delicious home-cooked meals. Yasmina and Amanda, you two are a constant source of inspiration for me, and I admire everything you do. Keep on keeping on! *Realiza tu sueño*!

DAVID, ALYSSA, JOSH, KRISTIN, DANNY, AND MY CRG FAMILY This book couldn't have happened without your support—thank you so much.

KELLY, LISA, LIZZIE, EMMA, JANE, ERIN, ALLISON, AND THE WHOLE TEAM AT TEN SPEED PRESS Thank you for believing in us.

Collaborating with you to create this book was a dream come true.

MARCELO AND REGINA Marcelo, you are a second brother to me. Thanks for the friendship we've had since we were seven years old.

ROB, A.K.A. "WILD BOAR" AND CHRISTINE BOONE You were my first friend at CHT and the most talented cook I've ever met! Thank you for always making me laugh! Christine, thank you for putting up with Wild Boar.

REGINALD "REGGIE" WATKINS EMPLOYEE #1 AT CHT Thank you for the beat down and the life lessons. Oatmeal beats no meal!

SARI AND SCOTT Sari, my first "boss" at CHT, I cherish our time together at CHT, and can't thank you enough for your guidance and expertise. Scott, you two make a dynamic duo!

THE DOMBKOSKIS My second family in Philly, thank you for being there for me. I will never forget the Sunday barbecue at the "funny farm."

DONA LEE TROTTER and the Trotter family. Charlie was a huge influence on my life. He taught me how to cook, but more importantly, he taught me to give. Thank you.

BETH, BRENT, MYRON, RACHEL, ELLIE, AND AVA, MY GREEN ACRES FAMILY I adore our friendship—thank you.

TRACEY, KATHY, AND EVERYONE AT THREE SISTERS GARDEN I respect you for what you do and thank you for your friendship, and Tracey, I greatly admire your talent as a chef.

LINDA, NICK, ZACH, AND JULIA Thanks for all your support.

KARENARMIJO What can I say? Thank you for your friendship, and one day we will get on a boat and do some real fishing!

MICHEL AND CLAUDE TOURNIER Thank you for your friendship and for guiding me through the restaurant world. Michel, you were my first mentor and will always be a father figure to me. You taught me a lot.

CHEF PIERRE POLLIN You taught me two lessons: Don't serve food that you wouldn't want to eat yourself. And second, and most important, always have time for family.

GEOFF AND CAROL Thanks for your friendship and for teaching me to never give up.

JACKIE, JANET, AND TIMMY We've made it through a lot; thank you for being my family.

HEATHER AND BRANDON Thanks to you both for all that you do! We will come visit you at "the Fox."

MINDY AND DAN Mindy, you are the best pastry chef in Chicago, even if I got to CHT first (and if you don't know, now you know!) Thanks for being such great friends.

MAWI AND ERIN Thank you for being my sounding board; I look up to you.

DON AND PAT Thank you for your friendship and the nights at the Pierini Palace. One day, Don, we will finally play that round of golf!

LIZ SORRENTINO Without you, this book would not have been possible, so thank you.

OUR CHEFS AND MANAGERS (DANNY, BEN, TED, DAE SUN, SARAH, KATE, MONICA, EDITH, SCOTT, JOSE, ELIZABETH), PREP TEAM AND COOKS, AND DISH TEAMS AT BELLYQ, URBANBELLY, AND BELLY SHACK Without the whole team, none of this would be possible—no restaurants, no retail sauces, no book. Thank you for all the hard work, long hours, and belief in the idea of no boundaries in cooking.

From Chandra

For my mother, Noreen Ram, who knows all about moving to a new country, exploring its food, and fearlessly cooking it with her own touches to bring family and friends together. Thank you for teaching me life's most important lessons. And to my husband, Jay Wilder, for your love and support.

Author Bios

Bill Kim, chef-author

Born in Seoul, South Korea, award-winning chef Bill Kim immigrated to the United States at age seven and found himself to be one of the few Korean kids in his Chicago school. He scrambled to assimilate, walking the fine line between fitting in with America and with his Korean family. His first formal kitchen duty—roasting sesame seeds and grinding them with a mortar and pestle for his mother's kimchi recipe—sparked his interest in pursuing a culinary career that eventually took him to chef positions in variety of restaurants, including Charlie Trotter's, Bouley Bakery, and Susanna Foo.

After spending years perfecting his skills alongside the best in the industry, Kim left fine dining in 2008 to venture out on his own, creating his own imaginative Asian-inspired cuisine with three highly acclaimed Chicago restaurants, Urbanbelly, which features creative and soul-satisfying noodle, dumpling, and rice dishes; bellyQ, a modern Asian barbecue concept; and Belly Shack, a tribute to his Korean roots and his wife's Puerto Rican heritage. Today, he is recognized as a pioneer in the movement of fine-dining chefs introducing casual concepts. Partnered with Cornerstone Restaurant Group and Michael Jordan, Kim reimagines Asian barbecue, amplifying it into a creatively modern and delicious interactive dining experience.

Chandra Ram, coauthor

A first-generation American, Chandra Ram spent fifteen years working as a server, cook, and consulting chef before turning to food writing and editing *Plate*, an award-winning food magazine. She holds a bachelor's degree in journalism from Loyola University Chicago, an associate's degree in culinary arts from The Culinary Institute of America, and has passed the certificate level of the Court of Master Sommeliers exam. She is the coauthor of *The Eiffel Tower Restaurant Cookbook* (Chronicle) and lives in Chicago with her husband, Jay Wilder, the world's most patient human being.

Index

Index